Who Bears the Tax Burden?

JOSEPH A. PECHMAN
and BENJAMIN A. OKNER

Studies of Government Finance

THE BROOKINGS INSTITUTION

WASHINGTON, D.C.

Library of Congress Cataloging in Publication Data:

Pechman, Joseph A   1918–
  Who bears the tax burden?

  (Studies of government finance)
  Includes bibliographical references.
    1. Taxation—United States.   I. Okner, Benjamin A.,
joint author.   II. Title.   III. Series: Brookings
Institution, Washington, D.C. National Committee on
Government Finance. Studies of government finance.
HJ2322.A3P4   336.2'00973   74-280
ISBN 0-8157-6968-7
ISBN 0-8157-6967-9 (pbk.)

9 8 7 6 5 4 3 2 1

Who Bears
the Tax Burden?

Studies of Government Finance
TITLES PUBLISHED

THE BROOKINGS INSTITUTION is an independent organization devoted to nonpartisan research, education, and publication in economics, government, foreign policy, and the social sciences generally. Its principal purposes are to aid in the development of sound public policies and to promote public understanding of issues of national importance.

The Institution was founded on December 8, 1927, to merge the activities of the Institute for Government Research, founded in 1916, the Institute of Economics, founded in 1922, and the Robert Brookings Graduate School of Economics and Government, founded in 1924.

The Board of Trustees is responsible for the general administration of the Institution, while the immediate direction of the policies, program, and staff is vested in the President, assisted by an advisory committee of the officers and staff. The by-laws of the Institution state, "It is the function of the Trustees to make possible the conduct of scientific research, and publication, under the most favorable conditions, and to safeguard the independence of the research staff in the pursuit of their studies and in the publication of the results of such studies. It is not a part of their function to determine, control, or influence the conduct of particular investigations or the conclusions reached."

The President bears final responsibility for the decision to publish a manuscript as a Brookings book or staff paper. In reaching his judgment on the competence, accuracy, and objectivity of each study, the President is advised by the director of the appropriate research program and weighs the views of a panel of expert outside readers who report to him in confidence on the quality of the work. Publication of a work signifies that it is deemed to be a competent treatment worthy of public consideration; such publication does not imply endorsement of conclusions or recommendations contained in the study.

The Institution maintains its position of neutrality on issues of public policy in order to safeguard the intellectual freedom of the staff. Hence interpretations or conclusions in Brookings publications should be understood to be solely those of the author or authors and should not be attributed to the Institution, to its trustees, officers, or other staff members, or to the organizations that support its research.

Foreword

In 1940 the Temporary National Economic Committee published the first serious attempt to estimate the distribution of federal, state, and local taxes by income class—*Who Pays the Taxes?* by Gerhard Colm and Helen Tarasov. Since then, a number of similar studies have been made, most notably one for 1948 by Richard A. Musgrave and several associates at the University of Michigan. In general, these studies were based on income distribution data obtained in household surveys. The taxes were then allocated by income class according to various assumptions about tax shifting. Frequently the income concept used to determine the distribution by income size was different from that used to allocate taxes. Moreover, the allocations were based on grouped data, which made it impossible to link income to tax payments of individual family units in the distribution.

This study is in the tradition of the Colm-Tarasov and Musgrave studies, with a number of modifications made possible by the use of computers. A tax estimate was made for each unit in a representative sample of 72,000 individuals and families. Care was taken to ensure that, when properly weighted, the incomes and taxes allocated to the sample units aggregated to the national totals.

Estimates were made not only for all family units but also for several significant demographic and economic subgroups. Perhaps most important, the study provides estimates of the distribution of tax burdens on the basis of eight sets of assumptions about tax incidence. The authors present the results of these different sets of assumptions but express no preference among them because there is as yet no conclusive empirical evidence on the incidence of some of the major taxes. The analysis is devoted entirely to the tax side of government budgets, and no attempt is made to distribute the benefits of government expenditures.

The estimates are based on income and taxes for 1966, the most recent year for which adequate data for such work now exist. There were structural changes in the federal income taxes in 1969 and 1971, payroll taxes have been raised almost annually, and many changes have been made in state and local taxes since 1966. However, it is the authors' opinion that the general pattern of tax burdens in a more recent year would not be very different from that shown in this study for 1966.

The data base used in the study is a microdata file that contains linked information from the 1967 Survey of Economic Opportunity (sponsored by the U.S. Office of Economic Opportunity) and the Internal Revenue Service file of individual income tax returns for 1966. These data do not, of course, reveal the identity of the persons to whom the information relates.

Many talented and imaginative computer programmers and research assistants worked on creating the data file and on the statistical analyses in this study. The key members of the programming group were Jon K. Peck and George Sadowsky, and the principal research assistants were Peter Gould, Andrew D. Pike, Ralph W. Tryon, and John Yinger. Others who contributed to the programming include Keith Beyler, Stephen W. Kidd, Robert Wallace, and Marjorie Odle. Norman S. Mauskopf, Michael McKee, and Carol Burke helped prepare the statistical material. Marcia Appel, Virginia E. Crum, and Kathryn P. Matheson carried the major secretarial burden.

The authors are grateful to the reading committee consisting of George F. Break, Robert J. Lampman, and Richard A. Musgrave, and to Robert D. Reischauer for numerous helpful comments on the manuscript. They also wish to acknowledge the helpful suggestions on Chapters 2 and 3 made by Henry J. Aaron, Michael Boskin, John

A. Brittain, Edward F. Denison, Arnold C. Harberger, Gerald R. Jantscher, Peter Mieszkowski, and Charles E. McLure, Jr. The manuscript was edited by Virginia C. Haaga.

The basic work on developing the tax file was begun under the Brookings program of Studies of Government Finance, which was financed by the Ford Foundation. The work on the distribution of tax burdens was financed by a grant from the U.S. Office of Economic Opportunity.

The views expressed in this book are those of the authors and should not be attributed to the trustees, officers, or other staff members of the Brookings Institution, the Ford Foundation, or the U.S. Office of Economic Opportunity.

KERMIT GORDON
President

February 1974
Washington, D.C.

Contents

Appendix Tables

Figures

CHAPTER ONE

Introduction and Summary

IN 1966 TOTAL TAXES paid by the nation's family units to the federal, state, and local governments amounted to more than $180 billion, or over 25 percent of total family income.[1] Strong views are held as to whether the burden of these taxes is distributed fairly by income class or among persons with substantially equal incomes. Some believe that the tax system is regressive; others consider it to be progressive.[2] Still others are concerned not only about the vertical equity of the tax system, but also about its horizontal equity. To a large extent, the debate has centered around the individual income tax, which is the largest source of government revenue in the United States. Even though the other taxes account for twice the revenue produced by the individual income tax, the distribution of these taxes by income classes is not generally known. The purpose of this study is to estimate

[1] This ratio is lower than the commonly cited ratio of government receipts to the national income primarily because taxes exclude receipts from nontax sources. See Chapter 2 and Appendix B for an explanation of the term "taxes" as used in this study.

[2] A tax is *regressive* when the ratio of tax to income falls as incomes rise; a tax is *proportional* when the ratio of tax to income is the same for all income classes; and a tax is *progressive* when the ratio of tax to income rises as incomes rise.

1

the effect of all U.S. taxes on the distribution of income by size of income and by other characteristics of the taxpaying population.

Major Features of the Study

Although others have made similar estimates,[3] this study is unique in two respects: First, the estimates are based on a microunit data file for a representative sample of seventy-two thousand families (referred to as the MERGE file);[4] when properly weighted, the sample accounts for the estimated total income received by household units in 1966. In addition to data on incomes, the file contains demographic and other economic information about each of the sample units (for example, homeownership, place of residence, age, and so on). This information is available on magnetic tape and can be processed quickly and efficiently on an electronic computer, thus permitting estimates to be prepared in more detail than was possible with the older data processing techniques.

Second, although progress has been made in recent years in improving the methodology of incidence analysis, economists still disagree about the incidence of several of the most important taxes in the tax system. Instead of limiting the analysis to one or a few views, estimates were prepared on the basis of eight sets of incidence assumptions that span the range of opinions currently held by economists. The estimates are of interest not only because of the differences, but also because of some of the similarities in the results.

The income concept used here corresponds closely to an economist's comprehensive definition of income for household units. In addition to the incomes earned in the production process (wages, interest, dividends, rents, and royalties), this concept includes transfer payments and capital gains accrued during the year (whether realized or not).[5] To convert income to a before-tax basis, indirect business taxes, as well as direct taxes, are included in income.[6]

---

[3] For a list of the most important studies of tax incidence, see Chapter 3, note 1.

[4] In this book, the term "families" refers both to individuals living alone (one-person families) and to the conventional Census family consisting of two or more persons, related by blood, marriage, or adoption.

[5] Gifts and bequests should also be included in income, but these were omitted because little is known about their distribution among household units.

[6] Direct taxes are automatically included in factor incomes; indirect taxes were allocated to individual family units in proportion to their shares of factor incomes.

The "incidence" of a tax—a term that is used synonymously with "tax burden" in this study—is measured by the reduction in real incomes that results from the imposition of that tax. Taxes affect real income in either or both of two ways. They may reduce the incomes of individuals in their role as producers; or they may increase the prices of consumer goods and thus reduce the purchasing power of a given amount of money income. The former effect is the burden of taxation on the "sources" of income; the latter is the burden on the "uses" of income. Both of these effects are measured in this study. However, no attempt is made to measure the burden that results from the reallocation of resources or of the changes in consumption patterns that may be caused by taxation. These effects are disregarded because they are believed to be small and are difficult to measure.

This book is concerned solely with the distribution of tax burdens, without any reference to the distribution of benefits from the governmental activities that are supported by taxes. It attempts to show how the distribution of disposable income under the 1966 tax system differed from what the distribution would have been if all tax revenues had come from a proportional income tax with the same yield.[7] This differential incidence approach was adopted because the benefits of many, if not most, government activities cannot be allocated even in principle.[8] Consequently, no inferences should be drawn about the overall incidence of government activities on the basis of the results reported in this book.

The remainder of this chapter summarizes the major findings of the study. Chapter 2 describes the basic concepts and methods, and Chapter 3 discusses the rationale of the different sets of assumptions used to distribute the various taxes to individual household units. Chapters 4 and 5 summarize the distribution of tax burdens by in-

---

For the rationale of this procedure, see Chapter 2, pages 19–20, and Chapter 3, pages 39–41.

[7] The differences between actual effective rates and the effective rate of a proportional income tax are not actually shown in any of the tables or figures in this study; they can easily be derived by subtraction.

[8] Many governmental activities produce "public goods" (for example, national defense), the benefits of which to any specific individual cannot be evaluated. For a discussion of the problems of measuring the benefits of government expenditures, see J. Margolis and H. Guitton (eds.), *Public Economics: An Analysis of Public Production and Consumption and Their Relations to the Private Sectors* (Macmillan, 1969).

FIGURE 1-1. Effective Rates of Federal, State, and Local Taxes under the Most and Least Progressive Incidence Variants, by Adjusted Family Income Class, 1966

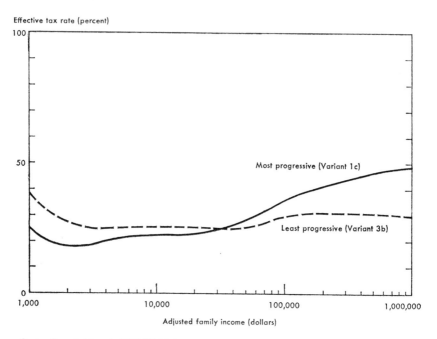

Effective tax rate (percent)

Most progressive (Variant 1c)

Least progressive (Variant 3b)

Adjusted family income (dollars)

Source: Computed from the 1966 MERGE data file. For an explanation of the incidence variants, see Table 3-1.

come classes and among various demographic and economic subgroups in the population. Detailed descriptions of the sources, the methods, and the basic statistical data developed for the study are given in the appendixes.

Summary of Findings

The major conclusions of this study may be seen in Figures 1-1 and 1-2. Each figure shows the effective rates of tax throughout the scale of incomes for the most progressive and the least progressive sets of incidence assumptions used. The only difference between the two figures is that the effective rates are plotted on a ratio scale by absolute income levels in Figure 1-1 and on an arithmetic scale by income percentiles in Figure 1-2.

Figure 1-1 gives the impression that there are large variations in

FIGURE 1-2. Effective Rates of Federal, State, and Local Taxes under the Most and Least Progressive Incidence Variants, by Population Percentile, 1966

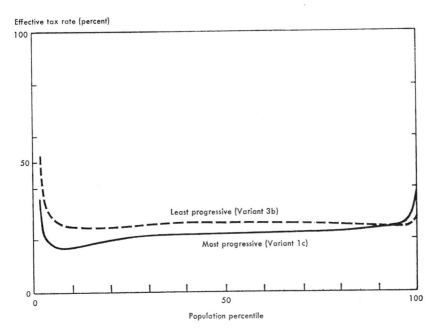

Effective tax rate (percent)

Least progressive (Variant 3b)

Most progressive (Variant 1c)

Population percentile

Source: Computed from the 1966 MERGE data file. For an explanation of the incidence variants, see Table 3-1

relative tax burdens between low and middle income recipients and between middle and high income recipients. Under both sets of assumptions, the tax burden is very high at the bottom of the income scale and then drops abruptly until the $3,000 income level is reached. Between $3,000 and $25,000, the effective rates range from 20 to 25 percent of income and then diverge above the $25,000 level. Under the most progressive set of assumptions (Variant 1c), the tax burden rises sharply until it reaches almost 50 percent of income for families with incomes of $1 million or more. Under the least progressive set of assumptions (Variant 3b), the tax burden reaches a maximum of only about 30 percent for those with incomes of $100,000 or more.

Figure 1-2 presents a different picture. Variant 1c is still more progressive than Variant 3b, but the difference between the two is much smaller over practically the entire income scale. Under each variant, there is very little difference in effective rates of tax between the tenth and ninety-seventh percentiles of family units. For this broad range of the income distribution, which covers incomes between $2,000 and $30,000 and includes 87 percent of all family units, the tax system is either proportional (Variant 3b) or slightly progressive (Variant 1c). At both ends of the distribution, the effective rates rise sharply, but the rise at the top is much more moderate under Variant 3b than under Variant 1c.

Because there is so little difference in effective rates over most of the income distribution, the tax system has very little effect on the relative distribution of income. This is illustrated in Figure 1-3, which shows the Lorenz curves for the distributions of income before and after taxes when they are allocated under Variant 1c assumptions.[9] As might be expected in the case of a progressive tax system, the Lorenz curve for the distribution of after-tax income under Variant 1c lies closer to the line of equal distribution than the before-tax curve. But the movement toward equality is relatively small—only 5 percent under Variant 1c and considerably smaller percentages under the other variants examined in this study. In the case of Variant 3b—the least progressive set of assumptions—the after-tax distribution differs only slightly from the before-tax distribution. This change is so small that the Lorenz curves for the two distributions cannot be distinguished on the scale used in Figure 1-3.

Variant 1c is more progressive than 3b largely because of differences in the treatment of the corporation income and property taxes. Under 1c, these two taxes are assumed to be taxes on income from capital,[10] while under 3b half the corporation income tax and the property tax on improvements are assumed to be paid by consumers through increases in the relative prices of housing and other goods and services.[11] Since property income is heavily concentrated among fam-

---

[9] A Lorenz curve shows the cumulative percentage of the aggregate income received by any given cumulative percentage of recipients arrayed by the size of their incomes. When all income recipients receive the same income, the Lorenz curve is a straight line with a 45-degree slope. As the distribution becomes more unequal, the Lorenz curve moves downward and to the right, away from the line of perfect equality.

[10] The assumption under Variant 1c is that half the corporation income tax is borne by corporate stockholders and the other half is borne by owners of capital in general.

[11] Under both variants, the individual income tax is assumed to be borne by the income recipients, sales taxes and excises are assumed to be paid by consumers, and employee payroll taxes are assumed to be paid by the workers. Other differences

FIGURE 1-3. Lorenz Curves of the Distributions of Adjusted Family Income before and after Federal, State, and Local Taxes, under the Most Progressive Incidence Variant, 1966

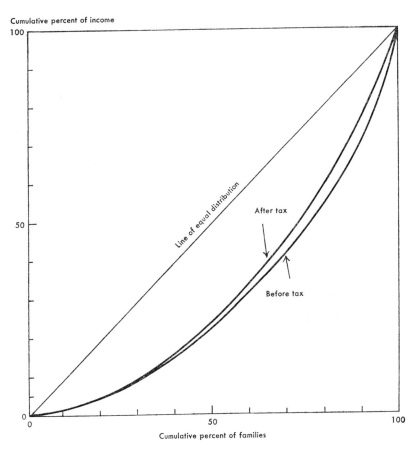

Source: Table 4-6. For an explanation of the incidence variants, see Table 3-1.

ilies in the highest income classes, effective tax rates under the Variant 1c assumptions rise sharply at the top of the income scale. On the other hand, the average effective rate of tax rises only moderately at the top under Variant 3b because the ratio of consumption to income

---

between the two variants are that the property tax on land is assumed to be paid by owners of capital in general under Variant 1c and by landowners under 3b, and that the employer payroll tax is borne by employees under 1c and shifted to the consumer under 3b. However, these differences have a relatively small effect on the distribution of tax burdens.

falls as incomes rise. Relative tax burdens under all the other variants examined in this study also depend heavily on the assumptions made with respect to the incidence of the corporation income tax and the property tax.

The high effective tax rates at the lower end of the income scale are probably due primarily to the use of a one-year accounting period for measuring income. When the accounting period is limited to a single year, there is a heavy concentration of retired-person families and of individuals with temporarily low incomes in these income classes. Such family units tend to consume more relative to their current incomes than do other units, so their consumption taxes are relatively higher. Taxes on property income are also relatively higher in these classes because families rely more on property income after the retirement of the main family earner than during the years in which he or she is working. Thus, the annual tax burdens shown in Figures 1-1 and 1-2 for the lowest income classes are probably not representative of the tax burdens of families whose incomes are low

FIGURE 1-4. Effective Federal Tax Rates under the Most and Least Progressive Incidence Variants, by Population Percentile, 1966

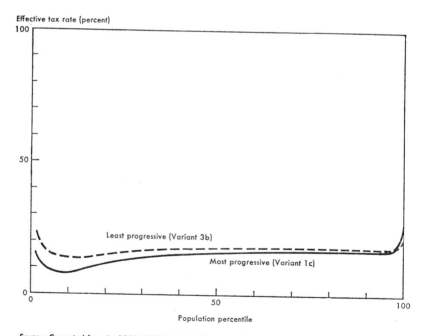

Source: Computed from the 1966 MERGE data file. For an explanation of the incidence variants, see Table 3-1.

when measured over longer periods. If computed on the basis of income for accounting periods of more than a year, the regressivity of taxes in these classes would be greatly moderated, if not completely eliminated.

The crucial nature of the assumptions as to the incidence of the corporation income and property taxes is also revealed when effective rates are shown separately for federal taxes and state-local taxes. (See Figures 1-4 and 1-5.) Because the federal government relies heavily on individual and corporation income taxes, average effective federal tax rates are mildly progressive throughout the income scale (except at the bottom, where the annual accounting period distorts real tax burdens). This pattern holds whether the corporation income tax is borne by owners of capital or is partly shifted to consumers. State-local tax rates are mildly regressive except at the very top, where the incidence of the property tax is controlling. If the property tax is regarded as a tax on income from capital (as in the case of Variant 1c), average effective state-local tax rates begin at about 20 percent

FIGURE 1-5. Effective State-Local Tax Rates under the Most and Least Progressive Incidence Variants, by Population Percentile, 1966

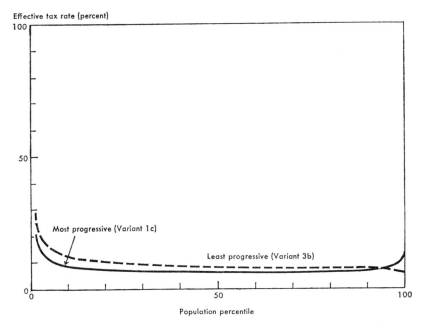

Source: Computed from the 1966 MERGE data file. For an explanation of the incidence variants, see Table 3-1

at the lowest income level, decline to about 6.5 percent for most of the income scale, and rise to 11 percent for the top incomes. If the property tax is regarded as a tax on the consumption of housing and of other goods and services (as in the case of Variant 3b), the burden of state-local taxes is regressive throughout the income scale. On this assumption, effective state-local tax rates begin at about 30 percent at the bottom of the income scale and decline to about 6 percent at the top.

In addition to differences that arise because of differences in incidence assumptions, there are substantial variations in tax rates among various economic and demographic groups in the population that are due to the structural features of the U.S. tax system. For example, homeowners pay lower taxes than do renters, urban residents pay somewhat higher taxes than residents of rural-farm areas, and married couples pay lower taxes than single persons.

The relative tax burdens imposed on income from labor and from capital also depend on the incidence assumptions for the corporation income and property taxes. If these taxes are assumed to be taxes on capital, income from capital bears a much heavier tax than income from labor. For example, under Variant 1c, the average tax rate on income from capital is 33.0 percent compared with 17.6 percent for income from labor. But the difference is narrowed considerably if the corporation income and property taxes are assumed to be paid in whole or in part by consumers. Thus, under Variant 3b, income from capital bears an average tax rate of 21.0 percent, while labor income bears a tax of 16.0 percent.[12]

In summary, the U.S. tax system is essentially proportional for the vast majority of families and therefore has little effect on the distribution of income. The very rich pay higher average effective tax rates than does the average family, but the difference is large only if the corporation income and property taxes are assumed to be borne by capital. If they are assumed to be shifted to consumers to a considerable degree, the very rich pay tax rates that are only moderately higher than average. Further research is urgently needed to resolve the question of the incidence of these important taxes.

---

[12] Labor and capital both bear a lower tax burden under Variant 3b than under 1c because the burden on consumption is higher—17.6 percent as compared with 8.3 percent.

CHAPTER TWO

Concepts and Methodology

THE FINDINGS PRESENTED in Chapter 1 depend on a large number of definitions and assumptions that were discussed there only very briefly. Because an accurate appraisal of the results and their implications requires a thorough understanding of what is being measured and compared, this chapter explains in some detail the concepts and methodology used in this study. The unique set of data for individual household units that was especially created for the study is also described.

Definition of Terms

To the average citizen, the terms "income" and "taxes" may seem self-explanatory. His income is the sum of the earnings he receives for his services and the return on the investment of his capital; taxes are the amounts he is obliged to pay to the government. These are also the definitions that the economist would apply in the case of most individuals. However, they ignore many complications that arise from the intricacies of a modern economy and of the government's relationship to the taxpayer.

Income

Economists define income as the amount an individual can spend during a particular time period and still have the same net assets (valued in money terms) at the end of the period as at the beginning. Another way of saying the same thing is that income is the amount of an individual's consumption outlays plus the increase (or minus the decrease) in his net worth during a particular time period.[1] Although this definition is almost universally accepted by economists, no government or private agency provides regular estimates of income on the basis of this concept.[2] The closest approach is the national income series published by the U.S. Department of Commerce.[3] Family income—the income measure from which the analysis in this study begins—was devised by the authors on the basis of the national income series.[4]

National income is the value, at factor costs, of the goods and services produced by the nation's economy. It includes employees' compensation, proprietors' income, net interest, net rental income of individuals, and corporate profits before taxes. Transfer payments, gifts and bequests, and increases in the value of capital assets would have to be added to make this concept correspond to the economists'

---

[1] See Henry C. Simons, *Personal Income Taxation: The Definition of Income as a Problem of Fiscal Policy* (University of Chicago Press, 1938), Chap. 2; J. R. Hicks, *Value and Capital: An Inquiry into Some Fundamental Principles of Economic Theory* (Oxford University Press, 1939), pp. 171–81; and Richard A. Musgrave, *The Theory of Public Finance: A Study in Public Economy* (McGraw-Hill, 1959), pp. 161–73. Outlays include tax payments on income as well as the taxes that are paid as part of the market price of consumption goods and services. In principle, an individual's net worth includes the value of human as well as physical capital; but changes in the value of human capital are excluded from this study because there are no data on the amount and distribution of human capital and because changes in the value of human capital are not generally regarded as an appropriate part of an income tax base.

[2] The authors of this study made such an estimate for the year 1972, with some modifications. See Joseph A. Pechman and Benjamin A. Okner, "Individual Income Tax Erosion by Income Classes," in *The Economics of Federal Subsidy Programs*, A Compendium of Papers submitted to the Joint Economic Committee, Part 1, *General Study Papers*, 92 Cong. 2 sess. (1972), pp. 13–40 (Brookings Reprint 230).

[3] U.S. Department of Commerce, Office of Business Economics, *National Income, 1954 Edition*, p. 58.

[4] As is noted below in this chapter and in Chapter 3, the appropriate concept for measuring tax burdens—which will be called "adjusted family income"—depends upon assumptions as to the incidence of the various taxes.

definition of income for a household unit.[5] As defined in this study, family income includes transfer payments and capital gains accrued during the year (whether realized or not), but does not include gifts and bequests because of the difficulty of estimating them reliably. (However, rough estimates of the distribution of income, including gifts and bequests, and of the effect of estate and gift taxes on the distribution of tax burdens are given in Appendix C.) In addition, since the analysis is confined to household units, income received by persons in the institutional population and by pension funds and nonprofit organizations and income retained by fiduciaries are excluded from family income.[6]

The national income accounts provide estimates of transfer payments,[7] but not of capital gains. Such gains were estimated separately for corporate stock and for other assets. In the case of corporate stock, it was assumed that the retained earnings of corporations—which are given in the national income accounts—are a rough approximation of the gains that accrued on their stock during the year. In other words, corporate retained earnings were substituted for realized capital gains reported on the tax returns of the family units in the sample. This approximation was used instead of the change in the value of corporate stock during the year because stock values fluctuate widely and even three-to-five-year averages may not give an adequate representation of accrued capital gains. However, Bailey and David have shown that over long periods of time, capital gains on corporate securities are roughly equal to retained earnings.[8] In the case of other assets, it was necessary to combine estimates of changes in the value of business inventories, farm assets, and nonfarm real estate. Changes in the

[5] Gifts are regarded as any other consumption outlay by the donor and are, therefore, not deductible in computing the donor's income. See Simons, *Personal Income Taxation*, pp. 57–58.

[6] The only other departure here from the official definition of national income is the omission of interest imputed to individuals for the services rendered to them by the banking system. For a more detailed description of the concept of family income, see Appendix A.

[7] Interest payments by the federal government are regarded as transfer payments in the national income accounts. Consequently, these were included in the transfer payments that were added to national income in deriving family income.

[8] See Martin J. Bailey, "Capital Gains and Income Taxation," in Arnold C. Harberger and Martin J. Bailey (eds.), *The Taxation of Income from Capital* (Brookings Institution, 1969); and Martin David, *Alternative Approaches to Capital Gains Taxation* (Brookings Institution, 1968), pp. 242–46.

value of business inventories are given in the national income accounts; changes in the value of farm assets and nonfarm real estate were estimated on the basis of other sources.[9]

The decision to approximate capital gains on corporate stock by the amount of retained corporate earnings means that family income includes all corporation profits before tax. In addition to retained earnings, these profits include dividends and corporate profits tax liabilities. Dividends are included in family income because they are direct receipts of household units; the corporation tax is included on the assumption that it is borne by stockholders;[10] and retained earnings are included as a measure of capital gains.[11] This procedure has the advantage of providing not only consistency with the concept of national income, but also a complete accounting of the accrued income claims of the household sector.

It should be noted that family income excludes some receipts that are usually regarded as income and includes some that are received in nonmoney form. Excluded are receipts from private pensions and annuities and government retirement benefits (such as civil service pensions) that are not financed through payroll taxes. Private and public employer contributions to funds for such benefits are considered part of family income during the year in which the contributions are made;[12] later, when payments are received, they are viewed as representing only a change in the form of asset holding by families. (That is, cash is increased, and a prepaid insurance asset is reduced.) On the other hand, payments to families financed through payroll taxes or general government revenue (for example, social security benefits and welfare payments) are considered transfers and are included in family income. Similarly, supplements to wages and salaries to finance health and other welfare benefits are counted as income in the year they are set aside by the employer and not in the

---

[9] For the method of estimation, see Appendix A.

[10] Under certain assumptions, the corporation tax is considered to be a tax on capital generally, on consumption, or on corporate wages and salaries. See Chapter 3.

[11] Corporate profits before tax are *not* adjusted for the change in the value of inventories. Such gains (or losses) on inventories correspond to capital gains and losses on other assets, which are included in family income.

[12] The federal government does not make current contributions to a fund for military retirement pay, but pays benefits out of general revenues when military personnel retire. An allowance for the accrued rights of such personnel was not made because no data were available for making an estimate.

TABLE 2-1. Summary of Derivation of Family Income from National Income, 1966

Billions of dollars

Description	Amount
National income (as defined in the national income accounts)	620.6
Additions to national income	
Transfer payments to persons[a]	56.3
Accrued capital gains on business inventories, farm assets, and nonfarm real estate	36.6
Total additions	92.9
Deductions from national income	
Income not received by family household population[b]	38.5
Imputed interest	15.2
Total deductions	53.8
Family income	659.8

Source: Appendix Table A-1. Details may not add to totals because of rounding.

[a] Includes net interest payments by the federal government and by consumers, which are regarded as transfer payments in the national income accounts.

[b] Includes income of persons in the military and institutional population and property income received by fiduciaries, pension funds, and nonprofit organizations.

year when the benefits are received.[13] The major forms of nonmoney income that are included in income are unrealized capital gains and net imputed rent on owner-occupied dwellings.

The derivation of family income from national income is shown in Table 2-1. In 1966, national income amounted to $620.6 billion. To build up this figure to an estimate of family income, it is necessary to add transfer payments of $56.3 billion and accrued capital gains on business inventories, farm assets, and nonfarm real estate of $36.6 billion. Income not received by families in the household sector and imputed interest, which amounted to $53.8 billion, are then subtracted, leaving family income of $659.8 billion.

Taxes

The definition of taxes in this study is basically the same as that of government receipts, as defined in the national income accounts.

---

[13] The model for this pattern of exclusion and inclusion is that of a private insurance system in which the equities of each individual are preserved. In fact, few private plans or plans for government employees are so designed, and benefits ultimately received by any particular employee bear little relation to the contributions made on his behalf. Moreover, benefits exceed the amounts originally set aside by the employers because of interest earnings on the contributions.

TABLE 2-2. Derivation of Federal, State, and Local Taxes from Total National Income Receipts, 1966

Billions of dollars

Description	Amount
Federal, state, and local government receipts[a]	**213.3**
Deductions for this study	
Personal and business nontax receipts	7.7
Corporate profits taxes of organizations not in household population	8.2
Nontax social insurance contribution receipts	7.8
Miscellaneous state and local receipts	0.3
Federal customs duties	1.9
Estate, gift, and death taxes	3.9
Total deductions	29.8
Federal, state, and local taxes (as defined for this study)	**183.5**

Sources: Appendix Tables B-1 and B-2.
a As defined in the national income accounts; adjusted to exclude the duplication of federal grants-in-aid to state and local governments.

However, since government receipts is a more comprehensive concept than taxes, nontax revenues were excluded from the tax measure. In addition, tax payments attributed to institutions or organizations not in the household population were excluded, and customs duties and estate and gift taxes were omitted from the tax concept. With minor exceptions, the procedure used here was to accept the national income accounts definitions for classifying tax and nontax receipts.[14] In 1966, total federal, state, and local government receipts amounted to $213.3 billion, while taxes as defined here were $183.5 billion. (See Table 2-2.)

Nontax receipts include personal and business nontax receipts, some items that are regarded as social insurance receipts in the national income accounts, and an assortment of state-local fees and licenses. Nontax receipts from individuals are primarily charges for tuition at state colleges and universities and local hospital fees, while nontax receipts from business include rents and royalties and an assortment of fees collected for various government services.[15] The

[14] The net receipts of government enterprises, such as profits from state liquor stores and public utilities, are also excluded from the tax concept used in this study, since these receipts are clearly payments for services rendered.

[15] An exception was made in the case of government receipts from persons for motor vehicle licenses. These were included in the tax concept (as is done in the national income accounts) even though this levy might be defined as a user charge.

excluded social insurance receipts are payments to civilian government retirement plans, which resemble private pension plans. They are omitted because payments into such plans are not taxes; they are regarded as payments on behalf of individuals for the purchase of future retirement benefits.[16] Miscellaneous receipts of state and local governments consist primarily of marriage license fees, charges for dog licenses, and similar items.

About one-fourth of all corporate stock is owned by fiduciaries and other organizations that are not represented in the family population. Total corporation tax accruals were reduced by $8.2 billion to reflect the amounts that are not borne by family units in the household sector.

The last group of adjustments—the exclusion of customs duties and estate and gift taxes—were made for special reasons. In the case of customs duties ($1.9 billion), the exclusion was based on the presumption that customs duties are levied primarily to discourage imports rather than to increase government income.[17] In the case of the estate and gift taxes ($3.9 billion), it obviously makes little sense to distribute death taxes among people who have died, since they no longer exist in the population. Logic would suggest that death and gift taxes be allocated among the new owners of the taxed property that was transferred. However, this would require that the amount of the gift or bequest upon which the tax was levied also be distributed among such persons. There is little statistical information available on families who received gifts or bequests in 1966 and therefore no reliable basis upon which to allocate either the assets transferred or the taxes collected.[18]

Total taxes by source for 1966 are shown in Table 2-3.[19] For all levels of government, personal taxes and payroll taxes on employers

---

[16] See page 14.

[17] The decision to exclude customs receipts from taxes is a close one. Since they amount to only about 1 percent of total tax receipts, the conclusions of this study would not be altered if they were included.

[18] Rough estimates of the effect of including estate and gift taxes are given in Appendix C.

[19] Not all taxes paid by families are actually collected from the U.S. household population. A small portion of personal income taxes is collected from families living outside the United States, and some sales and other indirect business taxes are paid by foreigners on goods that are sold abroad. No adjustment was made for these taxes because the amounts involved are small.

TABLE 2-3. Federal, State, and Local Taxes, by Source, 1966

Billions of dollars

Source	Federal taxes	State and local taxes	Total
Personal taxes	58.6	7.4	66.0
Income taxes	58.6	5.4	64.0
Motor vehicle licenses	. . .	1.1	1.1
Property taxes	. . .	0.8	0.8
Corporate profits taxes	24.4	1.7	26.1
Indirect business taxes	12.7	48.6	61.2
State-local general sales taxes	. . .	10.6	10.6
Gasoline excise taxes	2.9	4.8	7.7
Liquor excise taxes	4.0	1.0	5.0
Tobacco excise taxes	2.1	1.6	3.7
Other excise taxes	3.6	. . .	3.6
Motor vehicle licenses	. . .	1.1	1.1
Other taxes	. . .	4.9	4.9
Property taxes	. . .	24.6	24.6
Payroll taxes	30.0	0.3	30.3
Total	125.7	57.9	183.5

Sources: Appendix Tables B-1 and B-2. Details may not add to totals because of rounding.

and employees amount to about half of the $183.5 billion in total taxes. However, as is well known, state and local governments rely much more heavily on indirect business taxes (which include real estate property taxes) than does the federal government. For the lower levels of government, indirect business taxes accounted for 84 percent of total taxes paid by households, personal taxes were equal to 13 percent, and the other 3 percent was derived from corporate profits taxes. For the federal government, the distribution of revenue by source was quite different: 10 percent of total taxes paid by households came from indirect business taxes, 70 percent from personal income and payroll taxes (social insurance contributions), and almost 20 percent from the corporate profits tax.

Effective Tax Rates

Relative tax burdens are measured in this study by comparing effective rates of tax paid by family units. These are computed by expressing taxes paid as a percentage of income, and they thus reflect the proportion of the family's income that is accounted for by taxes. Although income is generally regarded as an acceptable measure, it should be noted that *income for a single year* (which may be unusually high or low) may be a poor indicator of "normal" financial status for many families. Current year income is used in this study for measuring tax burdens because income information for longer periods of time is not available.[20]

The income concept used for measuring effective tax rates is *not* family income as defined earlier in this chapter, but a concept derived from it called *adjusted family income.* This concept bears the same relationship to family income as net national product does to national income: adjusted family income is family income plus indirect business taxes. The relationship among the concepts of net national product, national income, family income, and adjusted family income is shown in Table 2-4.[21]

Adjusted family income is the most appropriate income concept for comparing tax burdens because it would be incorrect to compare burdens that include sales and excise taxes with an income concept that does not include these taxes. Since we are comparing tax burdens under several different shifting assumptions with reference to a proportional income tax, a consistent income basis must be used.[22] To achieve this, family income of all household units is increased proportionately by the ratio of indirect business taxes to family income, on the assumption that the use of indirect taxes does not alter the

[20] Relative tax burdens could also be measured by comparing taxes with family wealth (that is, net worth) or consumption. These comparisons are not made here because income is generally accepted as an appropriate measure of taxpaying ability. Moreover, data on family income are much more reliable than data on family wealth or consumption.

[21] In addition to the adjustment for indirect business taxes, business transfer payments and the statistical discrepancy are subtracted from the net national product, and subsidies less the current surplus of government enterprises are added to arrive at national income.

[22] For example, consider a country that produces total goods and services (net of depreciation) with a market price value of $1,000. Assume that it wishes to levy $200 in taxes and is considering two alternatives. Under alternative A, half the tax revenue would be derived from sales taxes and half from an income tax, while under alternative B, all the revenue would come from an income tax. In both cases, the real effective tax rate is 20 percent. However, with alternative A, national income (valued at factor costs) is $900 (the $1,000 of net product less $100 of indirect business taxes paid by consumers), while with alternative B, the national income (which includes taxes levied on the earnings of factors of production) is the full $1,000. Thus, unless indirect taxes are included in income, the tax burden would appear to be 22.2 percent under alternative A, as compared with 20 percent under alternative B.

TABLE 2-4. Relationship among Net National Product, National Income, Family Income, and Adjusted Family Income, 1966
Billions of dollars

Description	Amount
Net national product	685.9
Minus: Indirect business tax accruals and other adjustments[a]	65.3
Equals: National income	620.6
Plus: Net adjustments to arrive at family income[b]	39.2
Equals: Family income as derived from the national income accounts	659.8
Plus: Indirect business taxes[c]	61.2
Equals: Adjusted family income	721.0

Sources: Tables 2-1, 2-3; and *Survey of Current Business,* Vol. 50 (July 1970), Table 1.9.
[a] Includes business transfer payments, the statistical discrepancy, and subsidies less current surplus of government enterprises.
[b] See Table 2-1.
[c] Excludes customs duties and nontax receipts and includes other adjustments required for the distribution of tax burdens to household units. For an explanation of the other adjustments, see Chapter 3.

distribution of factor incomes. The resulting concept is the basis for measuring effective rates of tax throughout this book.[23]

Measurement Procedures

In the past, the income distribution data available for tax analysis have been deficient in two respects: first, they did not cover the entire income-receiving population, and second they failed to include all the income known to have been received by those who were covered. Annual data on income subject to tax, based on individual tax returns, are available from the U.S. Internal Revenue Service, but because data for people not required to file returns are not included, the distribution for those at the low end of the income scale is distorted. The U.S. Bureau of the Census also collects income information in its

[23] For an early discussion of this subject, see Tax Foundation, Inc., *The Tax Burden in Relation to National Income and Product,* Research Aid 4 (Tax Foundation, 1957). George A. Bishop examined the subject in detail in "Income Redistribution in the Framework of the National Income Accounts," *National Tax Journal,* Vol. 19 (December 1966), and concluded that indirect taxes should be allocated on the basis of the estimated benefits received by families from government, rather than on the basis of factor income. In a later study in which he participated, *Tax Burdens and Benefits of Government Expenditures by Income Class, 1961 and 1965* (Tax Foundation, 1967), indirect taxes were allocated on the basis of factor income—the basis used in this study—but the resulting income concept was not used to classify family units by income classes. The subject is also discussed by Musgrave in *Theory of Public Finance,* pp. 195–99.

Current Population Survey each year from a representative sample of about fifty thousand *households*. However, besides using a different population unit, the Census Bureau uses a *money income* concept—which includes nontaxable transfer payments, such as social security benefits, but excludes capital gains. In addition, neither the Internal Revenue nor the Census data contain any information on the distribution of nonmoney income and cannot be linked directly with the personal income or other aggregate statistics.

The lack of a consistent and comprehensive set of household income and tax data prompted the construction of a new microanalytic data base for use in this study—the 1966 MERGE file.[24] In creating the file, information on thirty thousand families and single persons included in the 1967 Survey of Economic Opportunity (SEO), which was conducted by the U.S. Bureau of the Census for the U.S. Office of Economic Opportunity, was combined with data from a file containing information from almost eighty-seven thousand federal individual income tax returns filed for the year 1966. Thus the MERGE file contains data for low-income SEO families, who are not in the tax-filing population, as well as the more complete—and more accurate—income tax information for higher-income individuals. In addition, income information in the MERGE file was corrected for nonreporting and underreporting, so that—with the appropriate weights applied to the sample units—the file accounts for the total income (on almost any desired definition of income) estimated to have been received in the United States in 1966.

Since the SEO income-reporting units are a sample of the entire U.S. population and the returns in the tax file are a sample only of the tax-filing population, the final MERGE file is based on the demographic information for the families in the SEO file. But income data from the tax file were substituted for the corresponding information in the SEO file to take advantage of the superior income reporting on tax returns (including the information on capital gains that is excluded from the SEO-Census income concept). This was done first by estimating, on the basis of reported SEO information, the kind of tax return or returns that would have been filed by members of each family and then, for tax filers, by matching each SEO tax unit with a return selected from the tax file.

---

[24] A detailed description of the methods used to create the MERGE file is given in Appendix A.

The ideal way to match the SEO data with the tax data would have been to obtain the tax information directly from the Internal Revenue Service. This was not possible because neither the Census Bureau nor the Internal Revenue Service permits others to use their files in this way, even for statistical purposes. Instead of using an exact match, a means of simulating a match was developed. A return (or returns) "similar" to the SEO return was randomly selected from the tax file, and income data from that record were substituted for the information in the SEO record. Since nearly thirty thousand matches had to be made, the selection and linking of returns in the SEO and tax files were performed on a computer.

For most families, the MERGE file contains the demographic data and information on receipts of nontaxable income from the SEO file plus taxable income figures from the return or returns assigned to it from the tax file. For SEO units deemed to be nonfilers, the MERGE file includes no federal individual income tax information. Since there are very few high-income units in the SEO file, the upper portion of the tax file (returns reporting incomes above $30,000) was substituted in total for the SEO file.[25] For this group, which represents less than 2 percent of the entire population, the MERGE file does not contain any SEO demographic data.

After substituting tax return data for the SEO income data, the total income not accounted for by the MERGE file amounted to 10 percent of total family income in 1966. (See Table 2-5.) The next step was to adjust the data in the file to correspond with national aggregates. As is indicated in Table 2-5, the aggregates for wages and salaries were close. But reported income of farm proprietors was 58 percent short of the expected amount, and there were less serious, but significant, discrepancies between the expected and reported amounts of interest, rent, and transfer payments. Some of the discrepancies were due to the partial coverage of the Census income concept, which was used in the field survey; the rest were due to nonreporting and underreporting of income by the survey respondents.

Where the discrepancies were believed to be due to underreporting, the MERGE file data were adjusted to the family income aggregates on the assumption that the underreporting was not related to other characteristics of the survey unit. A single ratio was therefore

[25] The dividing line was arbitrary; however, there is no obvious discontinuity or kink in the data at $30,000.

TABLE 2-5. Comparison of Family Income in the MERGE File and Income before Adjustment, by Source of Income, 1966

Dollar amounts in billions

			Difference	
Source	MERGE family income[a]	Family income before adjustment for non-reporting and underreporting[b]	Amount	As a percentage of MERGE family income
Wages, salaries, and other labor	$425.3	$397.4	$27.9	6.6
Nonfarm proprietors' income	44.5	39.4	5.1	11.5
Farm proprietors' income	12.0	6.9	5.1	42.5
Rental income	19.7	17.1	2.6	13.2
Corporate earnings	64.0[c]	55.8	8.2	12.8[c]
Interest	23.5	14.6	8.6	36.6
Transfer payments	34.2	26.2	8.0	23.4
Accrued capital gains on business inventories, farm assets, and nonfarm real estate	34.6	34.6	0	0
Total	657.8	592.0	65.8	10.0

Sources: Computed from the 1967 Survey of Economic Opportunity and 1966 MERGE data files.

a Figures shown are actual amounts recorded for family units in the MERGE file and differ slightly from control amounts shown in the text and appendixes.

b Unadjusted figures are based on data originally reported in the 1967 Survey of Economic Opportunity plus imputed income amounts not collected in the SEO but included in family income.

c Includes corporation income tax and undistributed profits.

applied to each category of reported income (that is, wages and salaries, proprietors' income, and so on) to increase them to the aggregate family income amounts. In the case of nonreporting, missing amounts were imputed to MERGE file units on the basis of various other characteristics of the survey units.

In addition to adjustments for underreporting and nonreporting, several imputations to the MERGE file were made to add income information that was not available—because it was not collected—in either the SEO or the tax files. These included imputed rent on owner-occupied homes, employer supplements to wage and salary income, tax-exempt interest on state and local bonds, interest on life insurance policies, and accrued capital gains on farm assets and nonfarm real estate. These items were imputed on the basis of characteristics of the survey units that were available in the MERGE file.[26]

[26] Thus, for example, accrued gains on capital assets were distributed among families on the basis of realized capital gains plus other property income reported on the returns in the tax file. See Appendix A for the methods used in making the other imputations to the file.

Since no information on consumption was collected in the SEO, the final step in preparing the MERGE file was to estimate consumption for each family in 1966. This was done by extrapolation from the 1960–61 Survey of Consumer Expenditures, conducted by the U.S. Bureau of Labor Statistics.[27] The 1966 consumption patterns (by item) were estimated on the basis of the age of family head, family size and composition, and the family's relative position in the income distribution.

[27] U.S. Bureau of Labor Statistics, "Consumer Expenditures and Income, Urban United States, 1960–61," BLS Report 237-38 (1964; processed).

CHAPTER THREE

Incidence Assumptions

PAST STUDIES of the distribution of tax burdens by income classes
have been based on a more or less standard set of assumptions as to
the incidence of the major taxes. The individual income tax was
assumed to be borne by those who paid it. Sales and excise taxes were
assumed to be borne by consumers of the taxed commodities. The
corporation income tax was assumed to be borne only in part by
stockholders; the remainder was allocated to consumers and, occa-
sionally, to corporate employees. The property tax on residences was
regarded as a tax on housing services, and the tax on commercial and
industrial buildings was assumed to be shifted to consumers. The
property tax on land was allocated to owners of land. Payroll taxes
imposed on employees were assumed to be borne by them, while
those imposed on employers were assumed to be shifted partly to
employees and partly to consumers.[1] For the most part, these assump-

---

[1] An early study along these lines was by Gerhard Colm and Helen Tarasov,
*Who Pays the Taxes? A Study Made for the Temporary National Economic Com-
mittee*, Monograph 3, Investigation of Concentration of Economic Power, 76 Cong.
3 sess. (1940). The classic study is by R. A. Musgrave and others, "Distribution of
Tax Payments by Income Groups: A Case Study for 1948," *National Tax Journal*,
Vol. 4 (March 1951). See also W. Irwin Gillespie, "Effect of Public Expenditures
on the Distribution of Income," in Richard A. Musgrave (ed.), *Essays in Fiscal
Federalism* (Brookings Institution, 1965); Roger A. Herriot and Herman P. Miller,
"The Taxes We Pay," *Conference Board Record*, Vol. 8 (May 1971); and Richard A.

tions were pragmatic compromises made by the analysts in the absence of a consensus among economists as to the incidence of the major taxes in the tax system.

During the past fifteen years, there has been a substantial change in the method used by economists to analyze tax incidence.[2] The distinguishing feature of this method is that it provides a consistent framework for the analysis of tax incidence, although it has not eliminated differences of opinion about the incidence of particular taxes. Nevertheless, important modifications are being made in the conclusions about the distribution of the burdens of some of the major taxes in the U.S. tax system.

This chapter summarizes the major elements of modern incidence theory, the conclusions that can be derived from it on the basis of alternative assumptions about the behavior of economic units, and the assumptions on which the calculations in this study are based. The study compares the distribution of tax burdens by income classes under eight sets of assumptions, without making a choice among them. The objectives of the calculations are, first, to determine whether it is possible to arrive at any broad conclusions about the distribution of tax burdens in this country whatever the correct assumptions may be; and, second, to illustrate the differences implied by the major competing views among economists about the incidence of particular taxes. The calculations do not provide any empirical evidence either to verify or to deny the validity of competing incidence assumptions or the analysis based on any particular set of assumptions.

Musgrave and Peggy B. Musgrave, *Public Finance in Theory and Practice* (McGraw-Hill, 1973), pp. 354–72. Only the Musgrave studies have provided estimates for alternative incidence assumptions.

[2] Musgrave, Harberger, and Rolph have played key roles in this development. See Richard A. Musgrave, *The Theory of Public Finance: A Study in Public Economy* (McGraw-Hill, 1959), Chap. 10; Arnold C. Harberger, "The Incidence of the Corporation Income Tax," *Journal of Political Economy,* Vol. 70 (June 1962); and Earl R. Rolph, *The Theory of Fiscal Economics* (University of California Press, 1954). Mieszkowski and McLure have also made significant contributions to an understanding of the new theory. See Peter M. Mieszkowski, "On the Theory of Tax Incidence," *Journal of Political Economy,* Vol. 75 (June 1967); Charles E. McLure, Jr., "Tax Incidence, Macroeconomic Policy, and Absolute Prices," *Quarterly Journal of Economics,* Vol. 84 (May 1970); and McLure, "The Theory of Tax Incidence with Imperfect Factor Mobility," *Finanzarchiv* (Tübingen), Vol. 30, No. 1 (1971).

Incidence Theory[3]

The current approach attempts to determine the incidence of a tax by following through its effects on (1) the incomes received by the producers of the taxed commodity or sector (the sources of funds) and (2) the consumption expenditures of individual households (the uses of funds). The burden of a tax on any household is the sum of the burdens borne by its members both as producers and as consumers.

Outline of Current Theory

The incidence of a tax depends on its impact on relative prices and relative factor incomes; its effect on absolute prices is indeterminate. Full employment is assumed to exist before and after a tax is introduced. Through its monetary and fiscal policies, the government can cause the general price level to rise, fall, or remain unchanged when a tax is increased or a new tax is imposed. Consequently the absolute price level is not relevant to incidence analysis. What is relevant is the effect of a tax on the distribution of *real* incomes that are available for private use; and this depends on the changes in relative product and factor prices and not on changes in absolute prices.[4]

The analysis assumes perfect competition, price flexibility, and perfect factor mobility. It also assumes that factors receive the value of their marginal products. While these assumptions may not hold for the short run, they are not unreasonable for the longer run, in which adjustments to changes in the relative prices of factors and in output prices may be expected to take place. In addition, the supplies of labor and of savings are assumed to be sufficiently inelastic with respect to changes in factor returns that they can be taken as fixed, even in the long run.

A tax will raise the price of the taxed product or factor relative to the prices of products or factors that are not taxed or are taxed at lower rates. Consequently, producers will tend to use less of a factor

---

[3] This section may be omitted by readers who are interested primarily in the statement of the incidence assumptions used in this study, which is presented in the next section.

[4] See Musgrave, *Theory of Public Finance,* pp. 364–65; McLure, "Tax Incidence"; and John A. Brittain, *The Payroll Tax for Social Security* (Brookings Institution, 1972), pp. 32–36, 53–55.

of production that is taxed more heavily; and consumers will tend to consume less of a commodity that is taxed more heavily. As a result of these relative price changes, a tax may cause a substantial shift of labor and capital among industries and in the consumption patterns of households.[5] These allocative effects may reduce the satisfaction of consumers of particular commodities, but they are disregarded in the analysis here—both because they are believed to be small relative to the total burden of most taxes and because they are difficult to measure.[6] What is left is the change in incomes earned by factors of production that results from the tax change and the change in the purchasing power of these incomes due to shifts in the relative prices of consumer goods and services.

Even if relative factor and product prices were changed by the imposition of a tax, there would be no change in relative real incomes if all households derived their incomes from the same sources and in the same proportions, and if their expenditure patterns were the same. In such cases, the burden of every tax would be proportional to income. The incidence question arises because changes in relative factor and product prices affect households at different income levels to different degrees.[7] However, often the uses side of income can be ignored because the expenditure patterns of those who are affected by the tax are similar,[8] or the sources of income side can be ignored because relative factor prices do not change.[9]

---

[5] A tax may also increase or decrease the nonmarket activities of persons in households. For example, a tax on money income or money consumption may encourage individuals to work less or spend less on goods offered in the marketplace and consume more leisure.

[6] Since it is assumed that the government follows a full employment policy, the tax will not reduce total income because its deflationary effect will be offset by appropriate fiscal and monetary policies. If the imposition of a tax is followed by increased unemployment, this is the result of poor government policy and should not be attributed to the tax itself.

[7] Inferences about the incidence of a tax cannot be based on changes in relative factor or product prices alone. Incidence depends also on the elasticities of demand for the taxed and untaxed commodities, elasticities of substitution between capital and labor, initial factor shares, and marginal propensities to consume.

[8] For example, as will be noted below, there is little reason to believe that there is a disproportionate consumption of labor-intensive products and services at one end of the income scale or of capital-intensive products and services at the other end. Hence, the burden of a general tax on labor or on capital on the uses side of household budgets can be ignored.

[9] Relative factor prices are unlikely to be changed by a general consumption tax or value added tax or when factor proportions in different industries are the same.

One of the major issues in incidence analysis is how to account for the uses of tax funds by the government. Clearly, relative factor earnings and product prices in the private economy may be altered as much by the way government spends its revenues as by the way it raises them. To avoid the need to trace through the effects of government expenditures as well as taxes on private incomes, some economists make the unrealistic assumption that the government spends the tax proceeds in the same way the money would have been spent by the taxpayers.[10] Others assume, more realistically, that substituting government spending for private spending does not significantly alter relative factor prices or the relative prices paid by consumers.[11] Still others address the problem by comparing the effects of two or more sets of taxes with the same yield. By assuming that government expenditures would be the same with either tax or set of taxes, the complication that might be brought about by different patterns of government spending is avoided.[12]

This study is based on the differential incidence approach, using a proportional income tax as the basis for comparison. The question it attempts to answer is: How does the distribution of disposable incomes of households under the present tax system differ from what it would be if the federal, state, and local government taxes they pay were collected through a proportional income tax with the same yield?[13] Each tax in the tax system is analyzed in this way, and the results are added together to arrive at the distributional impact of the entire tax system. The aggregate burdens are equal to the sum of the burdens of the individual taxes because each tax is compared with the same tax—a proportional income tax—with equal yield.[14]

[10] See, for example, Harberger, "Incidence of the Corporation Income Tax," p. 224.

[11] For example, it is probably true that the expenditures by social security recipients are not very different from the expenditures forgone by those who pay the payroll taxes that finance social security benefits. See Brittain, *Payroll Tax for Social Security*, p. 50.

[12] However, this involves other difficulties. In the first place, it takes it for granted that the marginal effect of the two taxes on the consumption of taxpayers with different liabilities under alternative tax systems is the same. Second, the *monetary* yield required to purchase the same assortment of goods and services may change if relative prices are affected by the tax change. See Musgrave, *Theory of Public Finance*, pp. 211–17.

[13] The reference tax is a proportional income tax that would apply, with no exemptions and deductions, to adjusted family income, as defined in Chapter 2.

[14] This technique was first used by Musgrave and others in "Distribution of Tax Payments by Income Groups," pp. 5–8, 37–39. For a more recent application of the

Implications of the Theory Based on the Competitive Model

The approach to incidence analysis that is based on the competitive model suggests the following conclusions about the incidence of the major taxes in the U.S. tax system:

1. The *individual income tax* probably is not shifted since workers and investors do not appear to change working hours or saving in response to changes in tax rates. Among all groups in the labor force there is evidence that labor force participation or hours of work may be affected by the income tax only in the case of young people and some women, and these groups account for a relatively small proportion of the total labor supplied.[15] The private saving rate when the economy is operating at or near full employment has been constant for many years, despite large changes in the total tax burden and in its composition.[16] If total hours worked and saving are relatively fixed, a tax on incomes must be borne by those on whom the tax is imposed. This is based on the presumption that imposing the tax does not change either the demand for, or the supply of, factors of production (because productivity is not altered by the tax) and that factor proportions thus remain unchanged. There is therefore no reason why purchasers should pay more for the same amount of capital or labor after a tax is imposed than before. Since the tax does not change relative product prices, there is no burden on the uses side of household budgets.[17]

---

technique, see Richard A. Musgrave, Karl E. Case, and Herman Leonard, "The Distribution of Fiscal Burdens and Benefits," Discussion Paper 319 (Harvard University, Institute of Economic Research, September 1973; processed), Table 10.

[15] See Marvin Kosters, "Effects of an Income Tax on Labor Supply," in Arnold C. Harberger and Martin J. Bailey (eds.), *The Taxation of Income from Capital* (Brookings Institution, 1969).

[16] See Edward F. Denison, "A Note on Private Saving," *Review of Economics and Statistics,* Vol. 40 (August 1958); and Paul A. David and John L. Scadding, "What You Always Wanted to Know About 'Denison's Law' But Were Afraid to Ask," Memorandum 129 (Stanford University, Center for Research in Economic Growth, rev. April 1972; processed). Warren E. Weber, in "The Effect of Interest Rates on Aggregate Consumption," *American Economic Review,* Vol. 60 (September 1970), finds that increases in interest rates *reduce* consumer saving. On the other hand, Colin Wright ("Saving and the Rate of Interest," in Harberger and Bailey [eds.], *The Taxation of Income from Capital*) finds that the interest elasticity of consumer saving ranges from 0.18 to 0.27. Neither Weber nor Wright estimates the effect of interest rates on total private saving.

[17] A progressive tax would reduce the demand for commodities consumed by the highest income groups relative to that for commodities consumed by lower in-

2. A *general sales tax* would be borne by consumers in proportion to their total expenditures, because the tax does not change relative prices and hence does not alter consumption patterns.[18] Excise taxes do change relative prices, thus burdening those who consume the commodities that are subject to tax. There is no burden on the sources-of-income side, however, because any labor or capital that may shift from the taxed industries ultimately receives approximately the same income when it is reemployed in the untaxed industries.

3. The *corporation income tax* depresses rates of return in the corporate sector when it is imposed, but this encourages some capital to move to the noncorporate sector, where rates of return after tax are initially higher. As the supply of capital in the noncorporate sector increases, rates of return decline there, and this continues until net returns after tax are the same in both sectors. Thus the after-tax earnings of all capital are reduced even though the corporation income tax is imposed only on capital employed in the corporate sector.[19] Furthermore, assuming that the total supply of saving is fixed, the earnings of labor remain unchanged, and capital bears the entire tax. The effect of the corporation income tax on the uses of income is ignored because there is no evidence that consumers in one income class spend proportionately more or less of their income on corporate products than do consumers in other income classes.[20]

---

come groups. This same type of change in spending patterns occurs as a result of the imposition of special excise taxes. As was noted earlier in this chapter, the effect of such changes is not taken into account in this analysis.

[18] If all income were consumed, the incidence of a general consumption tax and that of a proportional income tax would be identical. In such a case, the two taxes would be borne in proportion to the initial shares of each household in total income, and it would be meaningless to try to distinguish between burdens on the sources and those on the uses of income. If some income is saved, the incidence of the two taxes becomes distinct; the proportional income tax is then borne in proportion to income (the sources side), while the general consumption tax is borne in proportion to consumption (the uses side). See Mieszkowski, "On the Theory of Tax Incidence," p. 251.

[19] On the assumption that the total supply of saving in the economy as a whole is not affected by the after-tax rate of return, the before-tax rate of return for the economy as a whole is unchanged by the tax even though the before-tax rate of return in the corporate sector is, in the end, higher than that in the noncorporate sector.

[20] If saving is responsive to the rate of return on capital, the corporation income tax may well be shifted in part to labor in the long run. See Martin Feldstein, "Inci-

4. Since the supply of land is fixed, the *property tax on land* is borne by landowners when the tax is first levied or increased.[21] The *property tax on buildings* has approximately the same effect that the corporation income tax has on the sources of income.[22] If the total supply of saving (and therefore of investment) is not responsive to the rate of return, a partial or a general property tax on buildings is shifted to the owners of capital in general in the form of lower rates of return in a manner exactly parallel to that of the corporate tax.[23] On the uses side, the property tax raises the price of housing services and other goods and services produced in buildings, relative to other prices.[24] Since the proportion of total income spent on housing falls when income rises (with income measured on an annual basis), this would suggest that the burden of the property tax falls as family income rises. However, the elasticity of housing expenditures with respect to income is higher when households are classified on the basis of incomes over a period of years rather than one year.[25] Further-

---

dence of a Capital Income Tax in a Growing Economy with Variable Savings Rates," Discussion Paper 300 (Harvard University, Institute of Economic Research, June 1973; processed).

[21] As was explained above, when the supply of a particular factor is fixed, the owners of the factor must bear the tax. However, if the supply of land is variable, a land tax would increase the price of land, and consumers would bear at least part of the tax. See Peter Mieszkowski, "The Property Tax: An Excise Tax or a Profits Tax?" *Journal of Public Economics,* Vol. 1 (April 1972).

[22] This is true only of a uniform property tax. Since the property tax varies greatly among (and within) communities, the property tax has differential effects similar to those of variable excise taxes. (See Mieszkowski, "The Property Tax.") In this study, only the *average* property tax is allocated by income classes; the effects of property taxes that depart from the average are ignored.

[23] Like the corporation income tax, the property tax on buildings may well be shifted in part to labor if saving is elastic with respect to the rate of return in the long run. See Feldstein, "Incidence of a Capital Income Tax in a Growing Economy."

[24] If the property tax were perfectly general and the supply of saving were not responsive to the rate of return, the price of housing services would not rise relative to the price of other goods and services. However, the property tax on improvements is generally confined to buildings (it applies to equipment and inventories in only a few states), and thus it is not a general tax on capital in actual application. If it were a general capital tax, it would impose no differential burden on the uses side.

[25] The elasticity of expenditure for housing with respect to permanent income is in dispute. According to de Leeuw and Aaron, housing expenditures are roughly proportional to permanent income (that is, they have an elasticity of about 1.0). See Frank de Leeuw, "The Demand for Housing: A Review of Cross-Section Evidence," *Review of Economics and Statistics,* Vol. 53 (February 1971); and Henry J. Aaron, *Shelter and Subsidies: Who Benefits from Federal Housing Policies?* (Brookings

more, the difference among income levels in the impact of relative price changes is probably small even if the elasticity with respect to permanent income is less than 1.0—partly because there is evidence that the ratio of the value of capital to rental prices increases as rents increase[26] and partly because the property tax on commercial and industrial buildings is also reflected in the relative prices of goods consumed by families in the higher income classes.

5. Like the individual income tax, the *payroll tax* is assumed to be borne by workers because lower take-home pay as a result of the tax will not induce wage earners to withdraw from the labor force. In these circumstances, the same number of workers will be seeking the same number of jobs. Since workers are no more productive as a result of the imposition of the tax, employers have no reason to pay higher total compensation. With before-tax compensation the same, the payroll tax must be borne by workers.[27] This reasoning applies to payroll taxes levied on employers as well as to those levied on employees.[28]

Effects of Changing Assumptions

Although the framework of the above analysis is accepted by many economists, there is some skepticism about the conclusions, on the ground that the assumptions on which they are based are unrealistic.[29] Markets are not perfectly competitive, and labor and

Institution, 1972), pp. 212–13. However, estimates by Carliner, based on a panel of households over a four-year period, suggest that the elasticity is about 0.6–0.7 for owners and 0.5 for renters. See Geoffrey Carliner, "Income Elasticity of Housing Demand," *Review of Economics and Statistics,* Vol. 55 (November 1973), p. 531.

[26] George E. Peterson and Arthur P. Solomon, "Property Taxes and Populist Reform," *Public Interest,* No. 30 (Winter 1973).

[27] Even if labor responded to the payroll tax by working fewer hours or by withdrawing from the labor force, labor would not necessarily be able to shift the tax. Although wage rates might increase in these circumstances, employment would probably be reduced; and, under plausible assumptions concerning the elasticity of demand for labor, the aggregate wage bill would probably be reduced by at least as much as the tax proceeds. See Brittain, *The Payroll Tax for Social Security,* pp. 39–44 and 55–57.

[28] Most public finance experts believe that the economic effects of a payroll tax are the same whether it is levied on employers or employees. For an empirical verification that payroll taxes are borne by employees even when the tax is levied on employers, see *ibid.,* pp. 59 and 60–81.

[29] The implications of this view are discussed by the Musgraves in *Public Finance in Theory and Practice,* Chaps. 15–19.

capital are not necessarily mobile, even in the long run. Moreover, despite the empirical evidence, many economists find it hard to accept the proposition that taxation has very little effect on the supply of saving or on work effort. They contend that, on the basis of other assumptions, which they regard as more realistic, the results of this analysis must be modified—at least in the case of the corporation income tax, the property tax, and the employer payroll tax.[30]

• With regard to the *corporation income tax*, it is argued that there is no evidence that unincorporated business in the United States has grown at the expense of corporate business in response to increases in corporate taxes.[31] The corporate share of the national income originating in business enterprises rose—with only temporary interruptions—from 58 percent in 1929 to 68 percent in 1972.[32] Much of the increase came from the relative decline of farming, in which corporations are not important. But even in the rest of the economy there is no indication that corporate output has been reduced as a result of the post-World War II rates of corporate taxation. If capital does not move from the corporate to the noncorporate sector in response to the tax, the burden of the tax will fall entirely on the owners of corporate capital.[33] The U.S. national income accounts treat the corporation income tax as a direct tax on corporations and thus are consistent with the view that the tax is not shifted.[34]

Yet a different result is obtained if one believes that the corporation income tax affects corporate pricing and output decisions. The classical view is that the corporation income tax is not shifted in the short run,[35] whether business firms operate in competitive or in mo-

[30] It should be reemphasized that the authors do not necessarily agree with these assumptions or those discussed earlier, or with the implications drawn from them by various public finance experts.

[31] See Joseph A. Pechman, *Federal Tax Policy* (rev. ed., Brookings Institution, 1971), pp. 114–15.

[32] U.S. Department of Commerce, Office of Business Economics, *The National Income and Product Accounts of the United States, 1929–1965: Statistical Tables (1966)*, Table 1.13; and *Survey of Current Business*, Vol. 53 (July 1973), Table 1.13.

[33] This assumes that the *total* supply of saving remains unchanged. See page 31, note 19.

[34] For the treatment of the corporation income tax in the national income accounts, see U.S. Department of Commerce, Office of Business Economics, *National Income, 1954 Edition,* Table 38; and Office of Business Economics, *U.S. Income and Output* (1958), Table VII-19.

[35] The "short run" is a period that is too short for firms to adjust their capital to changing demand and supply conditions. The "long run" is a period in which the stock of capital can be adjusted.

nopolistic markets. The reasoning is as follows: maximum profits occur when the cost of producing an additional unit of output is equal to the additional revenue obtained from selling it. Assuming that the firm seeks to maximize its net profit, the level of output and prices that maximized profits before the tax was imposed will still maximize profits after the tax is imposed. Consequently, a corporation income tax should have no effect on pricing decisions.

The argument against this view is that today's markets are neither perfectly competitive nor perfectly monopolistic and that firms do not necessarily seek to maximize their profits. In such markets, business firms have the power to set their prices to cover what they regard as costs plus a margin for profits. The firms may treat the corporation income tax as an element of cost and raise their prices sufficiently to recover the tax. Alternatively, the firms may have a target rate of return on invested capital. If this rate of return is to be preserved after a tax is imposed, the tax must be shifted forward to consumers or backward to workers; or it may be shifted partly forward and partly backward.[36] Still another possibility is that the leading firms in an industry may raise their prices to recover the tax and the tax will merely form an "umbrella" that permits less efficient or marginal producers to survive.[37]

• The *property tax on buildings* could also be shifted to consumers in the form of higher prices in the same way that the corporation tax might be shifted; that is, to the extent that property owners do not try to maximize their profits and have sufficient market power, they may be able to increase rents when a property tax is imposed. Furthermore, doubts arise about the incidence of the property tax if

[36] See Marian Krzyzaniak and Richard A. Musgrave, *The Shifting of the Corporation Income Tax* (Johns Hopkins Press, 1963), pp. 1–3. This view has been vigorously debated among economists. For the opposing view, see Richard E. Slitor, "Corporate Tax Incidence: Economic Adjustments to Differentials under a Two-Tier Tax Structure," and Richard Goode, "Rates of Return, Income Shares, and Corporate Tax Incidence," both in Marian Krzyzaniak (ed.), *Effects of Corporation Income Tax* (Wayne State University Press, 1966); and John G. Cragg, Arnold C. Harberger, and Peter Mieszkowski, "Empirical Evidence on the Incidence of the Corporation Income Tax," *Journal of Political Economy,* Vol. 75 (December 1967) (Brookings Reprint 146). For a continuation of the debate, see Marian Krzyzaniak and Richard A. Musgrave, "Corporation Tax Shifting: A Response," *Journal of Political Economy,* Vol. 78 (July/August 1970); and in the same journal, Cragg, Harberger, and Mieszkowski, "Corporation Tax Shifting: Rejoinder."

[37] Committee for Economic Development, *Tax Reduction and Tax Reform— When and How* (CED, May 1957), pp. 24–25.

saving is responsive to rates of return. In these circumstances, the initial effect of imposing a property tax is to reduce the rates of return to owners of real estate; but this reduction will ultimately discourage new investment and reduce the supply of buildings. The result will be a rise in the prices of services that are produced by dwelling units. Thus, instead of resting on the owners of real estate, the burden of the property tax on residential buildings will be shifted to tenants. Owner-occupants—who in effect are renters of their own homes—will also bear the residential property tax, but as consumers of housing services and not as owners of dwelling units.[38] Similarly, the burden of the property tax on other buildings will not fall on their owners, but will be shifted to consumers in general. These assumptions are incorporated in the U.S. national income accounts, which treat state-local real estate taxes as indirect business taxes.[39]

• The proposition that the burden of the *property tax on unimproved land* falls on the owner when the tax is imposed or increased has been accepted by virtually every economist since Ricardo.[40] But even this proposition is being challenged by some economists who argue that, when a property tax is imposed on land and on reproducible capital simultaneously, investors who would otherwise have purchased land cannot obtain a higher rate of return by putting their funds to other uses. Hence, according to this view, a general property tax reduces the rates of return on all assets[41] and, like the corporation income tax, is borne by owners of capital in general.

[38] See Dick Netzer, *Economics of the Property Tax* (Brookings Institution, 1966), p. 36. The entire tax can be shifted in the form of higher prices in these circumstances only if the demand for housing services is perfectly inelastic or the supply of housing is perfectly elastic (that is, if housing can be produced at constant costs).

[39] The tax on land is also included in indirect business tax accruals in the accounts, but this decision was apparently based on the fact that the available data do not separate the tax on land from the tax on other real estate—rather than on the assumption that the tax is shifted.

[40] See David Ricardo, *On the Principles of Political Economy and Taxation*, Vol. 1 of Piero Sraffa (ed.), *The Works and Correspondence of David Ricardo* (Cambridge, England: Cambridge University Press, 1951), Chap. 10.

[41] Assume that the rate of interest is 10 percent and a tax of 1 percent is imposed on all capital. If a parcel of land was worth $100 before the tax was imposed, it yielded a rent of $10 a year. The tax will reduce the after-tax rent from $10 to $9; but, since the tax is general, the interest rate will fall from 10 percent to 9 percent, and the value of the land will remain unchanged at $100. Thus, the land tax is not capitalized and is paid out of rents. See Peter Mieszkowski, "A Critical Appraisal of Land Value Taxation" (May 1970; processed).

• The conclusion that all *payroll taxes* fall on wage earners is disputed by economists who do not accept the economic model on which that conclusion is based. According to the alternative view, it is unrealistic to assume perfectly rational behavior in labor markets and to take no account of the possible effect of collective bargaining agreements between large firms and large labor unions. Labor unions may succeed in inducing management to raise gross wages when a payroll tax is imposed or increased. If the firms have enough market power, they may be able to raise prices and thus shift at least part of the payroll tax to consumers. The share of labor in total national income will remain unchanged, but the prices of labor-intensive goods and services will rise relative to others.

Assumptions Used in This Study

The eight sets of assumptions used in the calculations in this study may be classified into three basic variants, each illustrating a major approach to incidence. The assumptions in each group were chosen to illustrate the effect of modifications in the incidence of one or more of the major taxes.[42] In all eight sets, it is assumed that the individual income tax is not shifted by the taxpayer and that general sales and excise taxes are borne by consumers in proportion to their consumption of the taxed items. The major differences among the sets relate to the incidence of the corporation, property, and payroll taxes. The variants and modifications are summarized in Table 3-1 and are described briefly below.

Variant 1 illustrates the distribution of tax burdens if one assumes that supplies of labor and capital are fixed and that there is perfect competition, price flexibility, and perfect factor mobility. Payroll taxes on both employers and employees are assumed to be borne by employees in proportion to their taxed earnings; the corporation income tax and the property tax on improvements are regarded as taxes on all property income and are distributed in proportion to the property income reported by each household. In Variant 1a, it is assumed further that the property tax on land is capitalized and is therefore borne by landowners in proportion to the value of land

---

[42] In some cases, the modifications are not strictly consistent with the basic rationale of the particular group of variants.

TABLE 3-1. Tax Incidence Assumptions Used in This Study

Tax and basis of allocation	Variant 1			Variant 2		Variant 3		
	a	b	c	a	b	a	b	c
Individual income tax								
To taxpayers	X	X	X	X	X	X	X	X
Sales and excise taxes								
To consumption of taxed commodities	X	X	X	X	X	X	X	X
Corporation income tax								
To dividends	...	...	...	X	X	...	...	...
To property income in general	X	X	...	...	...	...	...	...
Half to dividends; half to property income in general	...	...	X	...	...	...	...	X
Half to dividends; one-fourth to consumption; one-fourth to employee compensation	...	...	...	...	...	X	...	...
Half to property income in general; half to consumption	...	...	...	...	...	...	X	...
Property tax on land								
To landowners	X	...	...	X	X	X	X	X
To property income in general	...	X	X	...	...	...	...	...
Property tax on improvements								
To shelter and consumption	...	...	...	X	X	X	X	...
To property income in general	X	X	X	...	...	...	...	...
Half to shelter and consumption; half to property income in general	...	...	...	...	...	...	...	X
Payroll tax on employees								
To employee compensation	X	X	X	X	X	X	X	X
Payroll tax on employers								
To employee compensation	X	X	X	X	...	X	...	X
Half to employee compensation; half to consumption	...	...	...	...	X	...	X	...

owned.[43] In Variants 1b and 1c, the property tax on land is treated in the same way as the property tax on improvements (that is, it is allocated to property income in general). In addition, in Variant 1c, half the corporation income tax is assumed to be borne by stockholders and the other half by owners of property in general.

[43] Under this assumption, the present property tax was borne by the landowners when the property tax was first imposed and by those who were the owners when the tax was increased. Since these owners cannot now be identified, the property tax is allocated in this study to present landowners because they are the ones who would benefit from its removal.

In *Variant 2*, the corporation income tax is allocated to stock-holders in proportion to the dividends they received; the property tax on dwellings is allocated in proportion to the cash or imputed rent of households; and the property tax on commercial and industrial real estate is allocated to consumption in general. The two sets of assumptions in this variant differ with respect to the treatment of the payroll tax levied on employers. In Variant 2a, which follows the assumptions that are implicit in the U.S. national income accounts, the employer payroll tax is assumed to be borne by employees. In Variant 2b, half of the employer tax is assumed to be shifted to consumers[44] and the other half to be paid by employees.

Variant 3 presents several compromises among the views as to tax incidence represented in the other variants. Variant 3a allocates the corporation income tax among three groups: half to stockholders, one-fourth to consumers of corporate products, and the remaining fourth to corporate employees. In all other respects, this variant follows the national income accounts assumptions (Variant 2a). In Variant 3b, half the corporation income tax is allocated to consumers, and the remaining half is allocated to property income in general; in addition, half the payroll tax on employers is assumed to be shifted to consumers. In Variant 3c, half the corporation income tax is borne by stockholders and half by property income-recipients in general; the payroll tax is assumed to be borne entirely by employees; and half of the property tax on improvements is assumed to be borne by recipients of property income and the other half to be shifted in the form of higher prices for shelter and consumption goods.

Relation between Income and Taxes

Although it is not immediately obvious, the total amount of income of units in the household sector, as well as the taxes paid by them, depend on the incidence assumptions that are adopted with respect to the various taxes. Under the practice followed in the national income accounts, taxes borne by labor or capital are in-

---

[44] Strictly speaking, if the employer tax is shifted (see page 37), the tax is borne by consumers of labor-intensive goods and services. However, information on the consumption of labor-intensive goods relative to that of capital-intensive goods by income classes is not available. Accordingly, in this variant, the employer tax is allocated on the basis of total consumption.

cluded in the national income computed at factor costs. Indirect business tax accruals, which are assumed to be shifted to consumers, are included in the national income computed at market prices.[45] As was indicated in Chapter 2, "family income," as the term is used in this study, corresponds to the national income at factor costs, while "adjusted family income" corresponds to national income at market prices.

However, these relationships apply only under the incidence assumptions used in the national income accounts (Variant 2a). Whenever there is a departure from these assumptions (that is, when a tax is assumed to be borne by consumers rather than by labor or capital, or vice versa), family incomes and adjusted family incomes must be changed. The changes are required for two reasons: first, factor incomes are overstated in the national income accounts to the extent that the tax is shifted to consumers; and second, where taxes are borne by property owners, the amount of taxes allocated to the household sector will depend upon the proportion of total property income received by that sector.[46]

Since all eight sets of assumptions in Table 3-1 treat the individual income tax and sales and excise taxes in the same way, modifications in family income and in adjusted family income are needed to maintain consistency in the definitions of "income" and "taxes" only in the cases of the corporation income tax, the property tax, and the payroll tax.

• When the *corporation tax* is assumed to be borne entirely by stockholders, the tax is included in factor incomes and hence in family income. This is the procedure used in the national income accounts. However, if part or all of the corporation income tax is assumed to be borne by recipients of property income in general, that part must be subtracted from incomes obtained from the corporate sector and added to all property incomes. Similarly, if part or all of the corporation tax is assumed to be shifted forward to consumers, that part must be excluded from corporate incomes and added to indirect business taxes.

• In the national income accounts, the *property tax* is regarded as an indirect business tax. If all or part of the tax is regarded as a tax

---

[45] This is called *net national product* in the national income accounts.

[46] In making these adjustments, it is assumed that consumption patterns and factor shares are the same under the different incidence assumptions.

on property incomes, property incomes as measured in the national income accounts must be "grossed up" by the portion of the property tax that was not in factor incomes.

• *Employer and employee payroll taxes* are treated in the national income accounts as if both were borne by employees. If part or all of the payroll tax is assumed to be shifted forward to consumers, that part should be deducted from employee compensation and treated as an indirect business tax.

When a tax on labor or capital is assumed to be shifted forward to consumers, the amount of family income (as defined in this study) is reduced, but adjusted family income remains unchanged. However, in some cases the population affected by the tax is different under the two sets of assumptions. For example, if the corporation income tax is a tax on stockholders, the tax is allocated between financial institutions and stockholders in households, and only the tax borne by households is included in family income. On the other hand, if part of the corporation income tax is assumed to be shifted to consumers, that part is borne entirely by units in the household sector (since financial institutions do not make consumption expenditures). In this case, the shifted portion of the corporation income tax is excluded from family income, but it reappears as an indirect business tax in adjusted family income. In all cases, reductions and increases in family income are allocated among households in proportion to the income sources that are affected by the change. When a tax is distributed in proportion to property incomes in general, the allocation is made on the basis of property incomes *after* tax.

Table 3-2 summarizes the amounts of family income, adjusted family income, and taxes for each of the eight variants shown in Table 3-1. Although there are significant differences in aggregate family income among the variants, differences in adjusted family income—which reflect only the differences in the populations to which taxes were allocated—are relatively small. As a result, the differences in effective rates are small, ranging from a low of 25.4 percent (Variant 1c) to a high of 26.1 percent (Variant 3b).

While the differences in aggregate effective rates are small, the tax burdens of individual families may vary greatly under the several sets of incidence assumptions. All income and tax adjustments are carried through to individual family units, and the distributions by income classes reflect these adjustments. Thus, a family with an an-

TABLE 3-2. Family Income, Adjusted Family Income, Taxes, and Effective Rate of Tax under Various Incidence Assumptions, 1966

Dollar amounts in billions; tax rates in percent

Incidence assumption[a]	Family income	Adjusted family income	Total taxes	Effective rate of tax[b]
Variant 1a	$686.4	$723.1	$185.6	25.7
Variant 1b	685.5	722.2	184.7	25.6
Variant 1c	683.5	720.1	182.6	25.4
Variant 2a	667.3	721.0	183.5	25.5
Variant 2b	659.2	721.0	183.5	25.5
Variant 3a	662.8	725.1	187.7	25.9
Variant 3b	648.2	727.2	189.7	26.1
Variant 3c	676.9	722.0	184.6	25.6

Sources: Appendix Tables A-4 and B-6.
Note: Income and tax amounts are derived from aggregate control data and vary slightly from the actual amounts in the MERGE data file.
[a] For the assumptions under each variant, see Table 3-1.
[b] Based on adjusted family income.

nual income of $10,000 under one set of assumptions may be classified in a higher income class under another set and in a lower class under a third set. Families are also reclassified on the basis of the relevant adjusted family incomes in the relative income (percentile) distributions. Consequently, in examining effective tax rates for any income class under the several incidence variants, it should be noted that the income classification (whether on an absolute or on a relative basis) does not necessarily contain the same families under each variant.

Allocation of Taxes by Income Classes

Estimates of the 1966 taxes paid by each family unit in the MERGE file were made for each set of assumptions.[47] The federal individual income tax was carried over from the tax file. The portion of the corporation income tax borne by stockholders was distributed among families on the basis of dividend income; the portion borne by property incomes in general was distributed on the basis of property incomes after tax; and the portion shifted to consumers was distributed on the basis of total money consumption. Payroll taxes were

[47] Details of the methods used to estimate taxes for each unit are given in Appendix B.

estimated on the basis of the employment incomes reported in the MERGE file or, to the extent that the payroll taxes were shifted to consumers, on the basis of total money consumption. For other taxes, the information reported for persons who had itemized deductions on their federal income tax returns was used when it was available, and the remainder was estimated on the basis of other information in the file.

Since state-local income taxes, retail sales taxes, gasoline excises, and property taxes are allowed as itemized deductions in computing federal individual income tax liability, it was necessary to estimate these taxes only for families who did not itemize deductions or did not file tax returns in 1966. The same general allocation procedure was used for each tax. Total collections were first divided between the tax estimated to have been collected from business firms and the tax paid directly by households. The taxes paid by business were assumed to be shifted forward and were distributed among families in proportion to their total money consumption. The taxes paid directly by households were distributed among families that did not itemize—on the basis of their estimated consumption of the taxed items in the case of the specific excise taxes and on the basis of total money consumption in the case of the general sales taxes.

Because not all states had income taxes in 1966, it was necessary to select families that were subject to tax and did not itemize. This was done by assuming that the percentage of families paying state income taxes that did not itemize was the same as the percentage of the population in income tax states in 1966. The families were selected randomly, and the tax amounts were allocated on the basis of the reported taxes of itemizing families of similar size, composition, and income.

It was assumed that all real estate property taxes reported as itemized deductions were levied on owner-occupied dwellings. The amount not included in the itemized deductions was distributed among families that did not itemize deductions, or did not file returns, on the basis of the value of homes or rental payments. As was also the case with respect to the corporation income tax and the employment tax, property taxes were distributed differently under the various incidence assumptions.

CHAPTER FOUR

Distribution of Tax Burdens by Income Classes

THE MAJOR RESULTS of the calculations based on the eight sets of incidence assumptions described in Chapter 3 are presented in this and the following chapter. This chapter is concerned with the distribution of tax burdens for the population as a whole. Chapter 5 analyzes the relative tax burdens of various groups in the population.

Distribution of Income

The distribution of adjusted family income—the basic concept used in this study to classify family units by size of income—differs from other well-known distributions for two reasons: first, the incomes of the sample units in the MERGE file were adjusted upward, so that when properly weighted they add to the national income aggregates; and second, adjusted family income is a more comprehensive income concept than that used in previous studies. To illustrate the magnitudes involved, 1966 incomes for the population as a whole on the basis of six different income concepts are compared in Table 4-1.

Money factor income, which is the money income received by members of household units as wage or salary workers, entrepreneurs,

TABLE 4-1. Comparison of Average Income for Family Units under Six Different Concepts, 1966

Income concept	Number of family units[a] (millions)	Total income (billions of dollars)	Average family income (dollars)
Money factor income,[b] unadjusted	57.4	421.3	7,340
Money factor income,[b] adjusted	57.4	484.0	8,432
Money income,[c] unadjusted	60.9	459.3	7,542
Money income,[c] adjusted	60.9	536.2	8,805
Family income, as derived from national income accounts[d]	60.9	657.8	10,801
Adjusted family income[e]	60.9	719.3	11,811

Sources: Derived from Tables 2-4, 2-5, and Appendix A. Unadjusted figures are based on data originally reported in the 1967 Survey of Economic Opportunity. Adjusted figures are actual amounts recorded for family units in the MERGE data file; they differ slightly from control amounts shown in the text and appendixes.

[a] The number of family units with money income is 3.5 million larger than the number with factor income because that number of families received transfer payments but no factor income in 1966.

[b] Money factor income is the sum of wages and salaries, interest, dividends, rents and royalties, and farm and nonfarm proprietorship income.

[c] Money income is money factor income plus transfer payments.

[d] For the definition of family income, see Chapter 2.

[e] For the definition of adjusted family income, see Chapter 2. The amount shown is computed under the national income incidence assumptions (Variant 2a).

or owners of capital, averaged $7,340 in the original Survey of Economic Opportunity (SEO) for the income year 1966. When corrected to the national income aggregates, average annual money factor income amounted to $8,432. Similarly, average annual *money income*—which is the sum of factor income and transfer payments—increased from $7,542 to $8,805 after adjustment to the national income aggregates. The inclusion of wage supplements, accrued capital gains, imputed rent, and other adjustments to arrive at *family income*—the comprehensive income concept, which is derived from the national income computed at factor costs—increases average income to $10,801. Finally, the addition of indirect business taxes to obtain *adjusted family income*—the concept that corresponds to the national income computed at market prices—raises the average to $11,811. This is 61 percent more than the unadjusted money factor income and 57 percent greater than money income as originally reported in the SEO.

The adjustments for underreporting and nonreporting and broadening of the income concept have a dramatic effect on the distribution of income. In the original SEO, the poorest one-fifth of the families had incomes of less than $2,823 and received 4.3 percent of total

TABLE 4-2. Shares of Money Income and of Adjusted Family Income
Received by Each Fifth of Families, 1966

Families, ranked from lowest to highest income	Money income, unadjusted		Adjusted family income	
	Income range (dollars)	Percent of income received	Income range (dollars)	Percent of income received
Lowest fifth	Under 2,823	4.3	Under 4,038	3.7
Second fifth	2,823–5,416	11.3	4,038–7,679	9.9
Middle fifth	5,416–7,878	17.3	7,679–11,212	16.1
Fourth fifth	7,878–11,000	24.5	11,212–16,000	22.6
Highest fifth	11,000 and over	42.6	16,000 and over	47.9
Top 5 percent	16,922 and over	16.0	27,273 and over	22.1
Top 1 percent	28,333 and over	4.8	56,667 and over	10.5

Sources: Computed from the 1967 Survey of Economic Opportunity and the 1966 MERGE data file.
Note: Unadjusted money income is based on data originally reported in the Survey of Economic Opportunity.
Adjusted family income is corrected for underreporting and nonreporting, as well as for differences in concept.
(See Appendix A.) The adjusted family income distribution shown is based on the national income incidence assumptions (Variant 2a).

money income; the highest fifth of the families had incomes of $11,000 or more and received 42.6 percent of all income. After all the adjustments were made, the poorest fifth of the families had *adjusted family income* under $4,038 and received 3.7 percent of the total, while the highest fifth moved up to $16,000 and over and received 47.9 percent of the total. (See Table 4-2.)[1]

Although the upward shift can be seen throughout the income distribution, the effect is most pronounced at the top. Based on data collected in the original survey, the top 5 percent included families with incomes of $16,922 and over, and they received 16.0 percent of total money income. After adjustment, the top 5 percent included families with incomes of $27,273 or more, and this group received 22.1 percent of total adjusted family income. The share of total income received by the top 1 percent of all families increased from 4.8 percent before adjustment to 10.5 percent after adjustment. This large change in the income distribution results mainly from the addition of high-income family units that were omitted from the original SEO population and the inclusion of capital gains in adjusted family income.

The relationship between the original SEO money income distri-

---

[1] For this comparison, adjusted family income is computed under the national income incidence assumptions (Variant 2a).

FIGURE 4-1. Lorenz Curves of the Distribution of Money Income and of Adjusted Family Income, 1966

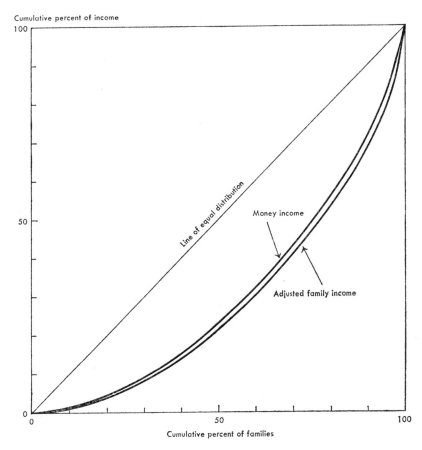

Source: Table 4-2.

bution and the distribution of adjusted family income is shown graphically in Figure 4-1, in which each distribution is represented by a Lorenz curve.[2] Clearly, there is a greater concentration of income at the top of the income scale when families are arrayed by size of adjusted family income rather than by size of money income. The degree of inequality, as measured by the Gini coefficients,[3] is much

[2] See Chapter 1, note 9, for an explanation of the Lorenz curve.

[3] The Gini coefficient is a measure of the equality or inequality in a distribution. It is the mean of all possible differences among the observations in a distribution, regardless of signs, divided by twice the mean of the distribution. It also equals the

greater for the distribution of adjusted family income. The Gini
coefficients are 0.4363 and 0.3871 for the Lorenz curves shown in
Figure 4-1.

Distribution of Tax Burdens

The distribution of tax burdens is usually presented by absolute
income levels, an arbitrary classification that tends to exaggerate the
significance of the data in some parts of the income distribution and
to diminish it in other parts. The MERGE file permits the tax burden
to be calculated by percentile groups as well as by absolute income
levels, and thus tax burdens can be compared for groups representing
the same number (or percentage) of family units in different parts of
the income scale. The pictures of relative tax burdens that emerge
from the two classifications are quite different.

Tax Burdens by Absolute Income Levels

Effective rates of federal, state, and local taxes for families at
different absolute income levels under each of the eight incidence
variants are shown in Table 4-3.[4] Except at the bottom and at the top
of the income scale, average tax burdens do not differ greatly under
the different variants. For example, the difference between the highest
and lowest tax rates is 2.7 percentage points in the $10,000–$15,000
income class and 2.1 percentage points in the $15,000–$20,000 class.
On the other hand, the average tax rates of those with incomes below
$3,000 and those with incomes above $100,000 show substantial
differences. Variant 1c, which distributes half the corporation income
tax to stockholders and half to property income recipients in general,
is the most progressive set of assumptions; the effective tax rate for
those with incomes under $3,000 under this variant is 18.7 percent.
Variant 3a, which distributes one-fourth of the corporate tax to wage

---

ratio of the area between the Lorenz curve and the 45-degree line (the line of equal
distribution) to the entire area below the 45-degree line. Its value varies from 0
(indicating perfect equality) to 1 (indicating perfect inequality). See Horst Menders-
hausen, *Changes in Income Distribution During the Great Depression* (National
Bureau of Economic Research, 1946), pp. 162–67.

[4] All figures in this book are presented in the form of effective rates or other
summary measures. Absolute amounts of tax and income for each variant are available in a separate appendix upon request.

TABLE 4-3. Effective Rates of Federal, State, and Local Taxes under Various Incidence Assumptions, by Adjusted Family Income Class, 1966

Income classes in thousands of dollars; tax rates in percent

Adjusted family income	Incidence variants							
	1a	1b	1c	2a	2b	3a	3b	3c
0–3	19.5	19.4	18.7	21.4	23.2	23.6	28.1	20.9
3–5	21.7	21.5	20.4	21.3	22.1	22.9	25.3	21.3
5–10	23.5	23.4	22.6	23.2	23.2	25.1	25.9	23.5
10–15	23.6	23.4	22.8	23.5	23.2	25.3	25.5	23.5
15–20	24.0	23.8	23.2	23.5	23.3	25.0	25.3	23.7
20–25	24.7	24.6	24.0	23.8	23.7	24.9	25.1	24.1
25–30	25.4	25.3	25.1	24.2	24.1	24.4	24.3	24.8
30–50	26.8	26.8	26.4	24.9	25.0	23.9	24.4	25.8
50–100	31.2	31.2	31.5	29.4	29.8	26.8	26.4	30.2
100–500	38.5	39.1	41.8	40.5	40.5	34.0	30.3	39.6
500–1,000	41.5	42.7	48.0	47.5	47.2	38.2	30.3	44.6
1,000 and over	41.2	42.9	49.3	49.3	48.8	38.5	29.0	45.7
All classes[a]	25.5	25.4	25.2	25.3	25.3	25.7	25.9	25.4

Source: Computed from the 1966 MERGE data file. For an explanation of the incidence variants, see Table 3-1.
[a] Includes negative incomes not shown separately.

earners and another fourth to consumption, is regressive at the lower end of the income distribution and only slightly progressive at the top; under this variant, the average effective tax rate for those in the lowest income class is 23.6 percent—almost 5 percentage points higher than under 1c. At the other end of the income scale, the average tax rate for families with incomes of $1 million or more is 49.3 percent for Variant 1c and 29.0 percent for 3b.[5]

Another example of the effect of different incidence assumptions can be seen by comparing the effective rates under Variants 2a and 2b. The assumptions for these two variants are virtually identical (see Table 3-1), differing only with respect to the payroll tax on employ-

---

[5] The reader should remember that, because adjusted family income depends upon the incidence assumptions, the families in each income class may not be the same under different variants. This avoids the distortion in effective rates of tax that would result from misclassification. The same kind of distortion occurs whenever other definitions of income are used to classify families. For example, effective tax rates that are calculated on the basis of money income as defined by the Bureau of the Census (which is considerably smaller than adjusted family income) exaggerate the tax burdens in the highest income classes.

ers. Variant 2a distributes the entire employer tax on the basis of employee compensation, while 2b distributes one-half of the employer
tax on the basis of consumption and the other half on the basis of
employee compensation. In 1966 the employer payroll tax amounted
to about $18.5 billion, so only $9.2 billion—about 5.5 percent of all
taxes—was distributed differently among family units under the two
variants. Since the amount involved is relatively small, the effective
tax rates under the two variants may be expected to differ only
slightly. But the effect is by no means negligible in the lowest income
class. Because families with very low annual incomes consume a very
large proportion of their incomes, such families are allocated a larger
share of the employer payroll tax under Variant 2b than is the case
under 2a. As a result, the effective tax rate for families with incomes
under $3,000 is 1.8 percentage points higher under Variant 2b than
under 2a. The differences are relatively small for incomes above this
level.

Perhaps the most significant aspect of the data in Table 4-3 is the
absence for most of the variants of the U-shaped pattern of rates found
in earlier tax burden studies. Almost universally such studies have
concluded that the combined burden of federal, state, and local taxes
is heaviest in the very bottom and top income classes and is lowest in
the middle.[6] It is clear from Table 4-3 that this conclusion depends
heavily on the incidence assumptions used. The effective rate curve
is distinctly U-shaped only under Variants 2b, 3a, and 3b. Under the
other five variants, the effective rates rise almost continuously
throughout the income scale.[7]

Tax Burdens by Percentiles

The effective tax rates under the eight different incidence variants
are shown in Table 4-4 for families classified by selected percentiles
in the income distribution. As can be seen in the table, under each
variant, effective tax rates are flat for virtually the entire population;

[6] See, for example, R. A. Musgrave and others, "Distribution of Tax Payments
by Income Groups: A Case Study for 1948," *National Tax Journal,* Vol. 4 (March
1951); and Roger A. Herriot and Herman P. Miller, "The Taxes We Pay," *Conference Board Record,* Vol. 8 (May 1971).

[7] Regressivity at the lower end of the income scale does not appear in the estimates for 1968 that were prepared by Richard A. Musgrave and Peggy B. Musgrave.
See their *Public Finance in Theory and Practice* (McGraw-Hill, 1973), pp. 365–72.

TABLE 4-4. Average Effective Rates of Federal, State, and Local Taxes for Selected Population Percentiles, Various Incidence Variants, 1966

Percent

Population percentile	Incidence variants							
	1a	1b	1c	2a	2b	3a	3b	3c
3d	24.3	24.1	24.4	31.5	33.8	31.9	35.6	29.2
5th	19.1	18.9	18.2	21.7	24.1	24.2	28.9	20.8
10th	18.3	18.3	17.4	18.9	20.5	21.0	25.4	18.9
20th	22.2	22.1	20.6	21.3	22.1	23.3	25.5	21.8
25th	23.1	22.9	21.6	22.1	22.6	24.3	26.4	22.9
30th	23.3	23.2	22.1	23.0	23.1	24.7	26.1	23.4
40th	23.4	23.1	22.7	23.1	23.2	24.7	25.7	23.3
50th	23.5	23.5	22.9	23.7	23.5	25.6	26.0	23.8
60th	23.5	23.3	22.7	23.5	23.2	25.3	25.6	23.5
70th	23.7	23.5	22.9	23.5	23.2	25.2	25.4	23.6
75th	23.7	23.5	23.0	23.5	23.2	25.2	25.4	23.6
80th	23.8	23.5	22.9	23.4	23.2	25.3	25.6	23.5
90th	24.6	24.4	24.0	23.9	23.7	24.9	25.0	24.1
91st	24.6	24.4	24.0	23.9	23.7	24.9	25.0	24.1
92nd	24.6	24.4	24.0	23.9	23.7	24.9	25.1	24.1
93d	24.9	24.9	23.9	23.7	23.6	24.8	25.3	24.2
94th	25.0	24.9	24.0	23.6	23.6	24.6	24.7	24.2
95th	25.0	24.9	24.5	23.7	23.5	24.3	24.1	24.4
96th	25.7	25.7	25.7	24.7	24.6	24.5	24.6	25.1
97th	25.6	25.6	25.2	24.2	24.2	23.8	24.0	24.7
98th	26.8	26.8	26.7	25.3	25.5	24.3	24.4	26.1
99th	29.2	29.1	28.3	25.9	26.2	24.1	25.2	27.5
Top	36.0	36.6	39.2	38.1	38.2	31.8	28.6	37.1

Source: Computed from the 1966 MERGE data file. For an explanation of the incidence variants, see Table 3-1.

they rise only in the very lowest and highest percentiles. For example, under Variant 1c—the most progressive set of assumptions—the average effective rate rises from 21.6 percent in the 25th percentile to 24.5 percent in the 95th percentile. Under Variant 3b—the least progressive set of assumptions—the average effective rate declines from 26.4 to 24.1 percent between the 25th and 95th percentiles. Moreover, the effective rates for all the variants are very close through practically the entire distribution. The maximum difference between effective rates among all the variants is only 4.8 percentage points at the 25th percentile, 3.1 points at the 50th percentile, 2.4 points at the 75th percentile, and 1.5 points at the 95th percentile. The differences are large only in the top percentile, where the effective rate is 39.2 percent under Variant 1c and 28.6 percent under 3b, a difference of 10.6 percentage points.

To aid the reader in interpreting Table 4-4, the adjusted family incomes corresponding to the lower and upper levels of selected percentiles are given in Table 4-5. The 20th percentile begins at about $3,900 of income for all the variants, while the 97th percentile begins at about $29,000.[8] As Table 4-4 indicates, tax burdens do not differ greatly in this very large range of incomes under any of the incidence variants.

Effect of the Accounting Period on Relative Tax Burdens

It will be noted that effective rates decline at the low end of the income scale in all variants when the population is classified by percentiles. (See Table 4-4.) This occurs at least in part because tax burdens computed on the basis of annual incomes are not representative of the burdens over longer periods at this end of the income distribution. Unfortunately, it is impossible to measure the extent of the distortion with the data that are now available. Nevertheless, the factors affecting relative tax burdens when they are measured on an annual basis are understood, and the direction of some, though not all, of these influences can be evaluated in qualitative terms.

A family unit will not ordinarily make its economic decisions on the basis of income in a single year. In particular, consumption and housing decisions—and the taxes paid in connection with such decisions—will depend on the economic status of the household over a longer time period.[9] As a consequence, the effective rates of tax based on income for a single year may not be representative of the tax burdens of families with unusually low (or high) incomes.

[8] Even though families may be classified in widely different percentiles under the incidence variants, the reclassification does not significantly alter the absolute income limits for any particular percentile of the income distribution. For example, the lowest adjusted family income for families in the 97th percentile ranges only from $29,000 under Variant 2a to $29,540 under several of the variants.

[9] The economic literature on this subject is large. See Robert Ferber, "Research on Household Behavior," in *Surveys of Economic Theory: Resource Allocation,* Prepared for the American Economic Association and the Royal Economic Society (St. Martin's Press and Macmillan, 1966), originally published in *American Economic Review,* Vol. 42 (March 1962).

TABLE 4-5. Absolute Adjusted Family Income Range for Selected Population Percentiles, 1966

Dollars

Population percentile	Incidence variants							
	1a	1b	1c	2a	2b	3a	3b	3c
5th	1,190–1,380	1,170–1,360	1,170–1,350	1,160–1,340	1,130–1,320	1,170–1,360	1,170–1,360	1,170–1,360
10th	2,120–2,290	2,120–2,290	2,080–2,250	2,070–2,230	2,050–2,220	2,100–2,270	2,120–2,300	2,100–2,270
20th	3,940–4,140	3,920–4,120	3,860–4,060	3,850–4,040	3,810–4,000	3,920–4,110	3,980–4,170	3,910–4,090
40th	7,580–7,750	7,560–7,740	7,490–7,670	7,490–7,670	7,460–7,640	7,650–7,840	7,700–7,880	7,540–7,720
60th	11,080–11,270	11,060–11,250	10,980–11,160	11,060–11,240	11,040–11,220	11,330–11,520	11,350–11,530	11,060–11,250
80th	15,820–16,150	15,790–16,120	15,630–15,970	15,720–16,050	15,720–16,050	16,120–16,440	16,190–16,520	15,750–16,080
90th	20,320–21,140	20,330–21,170	20,090–20,970	20,170–21,000	20,170–21,000	20,550–21,340	20,690–21,460	20,250–21,080
95th	25,330–27,000	25,330–27,000	25,170–26,830	25,000–26,820	25,170–26,830	25,310–26,850	25,570–27,000	25,170–26,830
97th	29,540–34,090	29,540–34,090	29,540–34,090	29,000–34,000	29,540–34,090	29,090–33,640	29,540–34,090	29,540–34,090

Source: Computed from the 1966 MERGE data file. For an explanation of the incidence variants, see Table 3-1.

Income in a single year may not reflect the taxpayer's longer-run economic status for a number of reasons: (1) Earnings may be unusually low during a particular year as a result of unemployment, illness, or other factors leading to the interruption of work. (2) Adjusted family income is frequently much lower than the flow of receipts available to families of retired workers. For example, receipts from pension plans and annuities are to a large extent conversions into cash of assets accumulated from income in earlier years. The retired worker's family is likely to make its consumption decisions on the basis of its retirement benefits, even though only a small fraction of the benefits is income as defined by economists.[10] And (3) income from many pursuits fluctuates over a period of years due to cyclical or other influences. There is evidence in the MERGE file that many family units suffer business losses that greatly reduce the amount of their total income and frequently result in negative incomes.

Taxes paid in a single year do not depend entirely on the income actually earned in that year. In many cases, a family continues to consume at a level commensurate with its longer-run income and, especially in the case of retired families, on the basis of accumulated wealth as well as of income. The taxes that are affected by these factors are consumption and property taxes. For the family units involved, the ratio of these taxes to incomes is much higher on the basis of annual income than on the basis of income over a longer time. Moreover, the differences are largest in the lowest income classes, where retired persons as well as family units with temporarily low incomes are concentrated.[11]

Some economists believe that consumption and housing expenditures, which tend to decline with income when measured on an annual basis, may be proportional to income when measured over a period of several years.[12] If this were the case, taxes on consumption and hous-

---

[10] For the definition of adjusted family income, see pages 19–20.

[11] Annual incomes also vary substantially at the top income levels; but, at these levels, the effect of income variability on the effective rates of consumption and property taxes is likely to be small because the ratio of consumption and housing expenditures to income is small.

[12] For consumption in general, see Milton Friedman, *A Theory of the Consumption Function* (Princeton University Press for the National Bureau of Economic Research, 1957). For housing expenditures, see Henry J. Aaron, *Shelter and Subsidies: Who Benefits from Federal Housing Policies?* (Brookings Institution, 1972), pp. 212–13.

ing would be proportional to income rather than regressive. Even if regressivity were not entirely eliminated, it seems clear that it would be much less pronounced over the longer run.[13]

The regressivity of total tax burdens found in the lower percentiles of the income distribution under all the incidence variants results primarily from the regressivity of the sales and excise taxes and of the property taxes. Whether the regressivity of these taxes with respect to income would remain for accounting periods longer than one year is not known. It seems clear, however, that the regressivity shown at the lowest income levels on the basis of annual figures would be greatly moderated, if not completely eliminated, over the longer period.

The Effect of Taxes on the Distribution of Income

Since the national tax structure appears to be proportional for a large segment of the population, it cannot have a significant effect on the distribution of income. When the before-tax and after-tax income distributions are expressed as Lorenz curves, the two curves are virtually indistinguishable. The cumulative percentages of income before and after tax are shown, by deciles, for the most progressive and the least progressive sets of incidence assumptions (Variants 1c and 3b, respectively) in Table 4-6. Although these variants depict the extremes, the after-tax percentages are clearly very close to the before-tax percentages. The effects of taxes under the other incidence variants on the cumulative percentages of income are also very small.

To illustrate the effect of the tax structure on the distribution of income in quantitative terms, Gini coefficients of inequality for the before-tax and after-tax distributions under the eight incidence variants are presented in Table 4-7. The after-tax Gini coefficients for all variants are less than the coefficients computed for the before-tax distributions of income, indicating that the tax system is on balance progressive on these sets of assumptions. For Variant 3b, which is the least progressive set of assumptions, the after-tax Gini coefficient is only very slightly lower than the before-tax coefficient. But the degree

---

[13] Multiyear data on consumption and housing outlays are not available for the very high income classes in the distributions prepared on the basis of the MERGE file for this study. It is doubtful that the alleged proportionality of consumption and housing outlays to income over a period of years extends into the top income classes.

TABLE 4-6. Cumulative Distribution of Adjusted Family Income before and after Federal, State, and Local Taxes, by Population Decile, Variants 1c and 3b, 1966

| | Cumulative percentages of adjusted family income | | | |
| | Variant 1c | | Variant 3b | |
Population decile	Before tax	After tax	Before tax	After tax
First	1.21	1.33	1.25	1.27
Second	3.88	4.34	3.98	4.08
Third	8.13	8.80	8.29	8.45
Fourth	13.92	14.65	14.15	14.22
Fifth	21.16	22.15	21.56	21.65
Sixth	30.22	31.03	30.85	30.48
Seventh	40.02	41.62	41.01	41.06
Eighth	52.29	54.31	53.44	53.69
Ninth	67.45	69.51	68.92	68.95
Tenth	100.00	100.00	100.00	100.00

Source: Computed from the 1966 MERGE data file. For an explanation of the incidence variants, see Table 3-1.
Notes: Variant 1c is the most progressive and 3b the least progressive set of incidence assumptions examined in this study. The cumulative percentages are based on distributions of family units ranked by their before-tax incomes and then reranked by their after-tax incomes.

TABLE 4-7. Gini Coefficients for the Distributions of Income before and after Taxes, 1966

| | Gini coefficient[a] | | Percentage decrease[b] in area of inequality |
Incidence variant	Before-tax income distribution	After-tax income distribution	
1a	0.4321	0.4156	−3.82
1b	0.4329	0.4156	−4.00
1c	0.4367	0.4158	−4.79
2a	0.4363	0.4192	−3.92
2b	0.4375	0.4217	−3.61
3a	0.4277	0.4203	−1.73
3b	0.4252	0.4240	−0.28
3c	0.4340	0.4171	−3.89

Source: Computed from the 1966 MERGE data file. For an explanation of the incidence variants, see Table 3-1.
Note: The Gini coefficients are based on distributions of family incomes ranked by their before-tax incomes and then reranked by their after-tax incomes.
[a] The Gini coefficient is the ratio of the area between a Lorenz curve and the 45-degree line (the line of equal distribution) to the entire area below the 45-degree line.
[b] Reductions in the Gini coefficient indicate decreasing inequality.

of redistribution is small under all variants, ranging from a low of 0.3 percent to a maximum of 4.8 percent.[14] As measured by the percentage reductions in the area of inequality in the Lorenz curve diagram, Variants 1c and 3b are again the most progressive and the least progressive sets of assumptions, respectively.[15]

Tax Burdens by Type of Tax

The tax burdens presented thus far in this chapter are the weighted averages of many different taxes. Some are progressive, others are regressive, and still others are progressive in some ranges of income and regressive in others. This section examines the contribution of the major taxes in the tax system to tax burdens at different income levels and by deciles under Variants 1c and 3b. Among the eight sets of incidence assumptions examined in this study, the former variant produces the most progressive distribution of tax burdens and the latter produces a slightly regressive distribution. Hence, the distributions of tax burdens under these variants represent the extremes resulting from different incidence assumptions.

The *individual income tax* is distributed in the same way under both sets of incidence assumptions. (See Table 3-1.) Revenue from this source accounts for about one-third of all 1966 taxes, and this obviously has an important influence on the distribution of tax burdens. The individual income tax is progressive over virtually the entire income scale, but it becomes regressive at the very top. This pattern reflects the fact that in the highest income classes a rising portion of total income as defined in this study is not subject to income tax at either the federal or the state level.[16] The individual income tax

[14] The percentage change in the area of inequality in a Lorenz curve diagram is derived from the Gini coefficients. Graphically it is equal to the percentage by which the area between the 45-degree line and the Lorenz curve is reduced or increased.

[15] The rankings of the variants as to progressivity are based on paired comparisons between the before-tax and after-tax Gini coefficients for each variant, rather than on a comparison of the after-tax coefficients. Only the first comparison provides a basis for making a judgment as to the distributional effects of the various sets of incidence assumptions. The rankings based on the second comparison depend on the before-tax distributions as well as on the effect of the incidence assumptions.

[16] For a detailed discussion of the items that are not subject to the federal income tax, see Joseph A. Pechman and Benjamin A. Okner, "Individual Income Tax Ero-

imposes the heaviest burden—15.3 percent of adjusted family income under Variant 1c and 18.0 percent under 3b—on incomes between $100,000 and $500,000. (See Table 4-8.)

The differences in the effective rates of individual income tax at the same income level are due entirely to the different definitions of income used in the two sets of assumptions. Under Variant 1c, the corporation income tax and the property tax on improvements are included in adjusted family incomes of stockholders and property income recipients; under Variant 3b, half the corporation income tax and the entire property tax on improvements are regarded as indirect taxes and are distributed among all family units in calculating adjusted family income.[17] As a consequence, stockholders and property income recipients have much higher adjusted family incomes under Variant 1c than under 3b, and the burden of the individual income tax relative to incomes at the top of the income scale (where dividends and other property incomes are large) is reduced.

Sales and excise taxes are clearly regressive throughout the entire income scale. They begin at over 9 percent of income at the bottom and decline to about 1 percent at the top, reflecting the fact that the proportion of family income spent on goods and services subject to tax falls as income rises. The small differences in the effective rates of these taxes at particular income levels also reflect the different definitions of income used in the two variants.

Payroll taxes are progressive for families with incomes up to about the $10,000 level, where they reach a maximum of about 6 percent and then become regressive. The progressivity of payroll taxes at the lower end of the income scale reflects two facts: (1) a large proportion of income received by very low-income units—mainly transfer payments—is not subject to these taxes; and (2) many low-income workers are in jobs that are not covered by the employment tax system. Payroll taxes are regressive above $10,000 because they are levied at a flat rate up to a maximum amount of annual taxable earnings; above this level, the tax accounts for a declining percentage of income. In Variant 3b half of the employer payroll tax is assumed to

---

sion by Income Classes," in *The Economics of Federal Subsidy Programs,* A Compendium of Papers submitted to the Joint Economic Committee, Part 1, *General Study Papers,* 92 Cong. 2 sess. (1972) (Brookings Reprint 230).

[17] See the discussion of the relation between the tax concept and the definition of income in Chapter 3.

TABLE 4-8. Effective Rates of Federal, State, and Local Taxes, by Type of Tax, Variants 1c and 3b, by Adjusted Family Income Class, 1966

Income classes in thousands of dollars; tax rates in percent

Adjusted family income	Indi- vidual income tax	Corpo- ration income tax	Property tax	Sales and excise taxes	Payroll taxes	Personal property and motor vehicle taxes	Total taxes
			Variant 1c				
0–3	1.4	2.1	2.5	9.4	2.9	0.4	18.7
3–5	3.1	2.2	2.7	7.4	4.6	0.4	20.4
5–10	5.8	1.8	2.0	6.5	6.1	0.4	22.6
10–15	7.6	1.6	1.7	5.8	5.8	0.3	22.8
15–20	8.7	2.0	2.0	5.2	5.0	0.3	23.2
20–25	9.2	3.0	2.6	4.6	4.3	0.2	24.0
25–30	9.3	4.6	3.7	4.0	3.3	0.2	25.1
30–50	10.4	5.8	4.5	3.4	2.2	0.1	26.4
50–100	13.4	8.8	6.2	2.4	0.7	0.1	31.5
100–500	15.3	16.5	8.2	1.5	0.3	0.1	41.8
500–1,000	14.1	23.0	9.6	1.1	0.1	0.2	48.0
1,000 and over	12.4	25.7	10.1	1.0	ᵃ	0.1	49.3
All classesᵇ	8.5	3.9	3.0	5.1	4.4	0.3	25.2
			Variant 3b				
0–3	1.2	6.1	6.5	9.2	4.6	0.4	28.1
3–5	2.8	5.3	4.8	7.1	4.9	0.4	25.3
5–10	5.5	4.3	3.6	6.4	5.7	0.3	25.9
10–15	7.2	3.8	3.2	5.6	5.3	0.3	25.5
15–20	8.2	3.8	3.2	5.1	4.7	0.3	25.3
20–25	9.1	4.0	3.1	4.6	4.1	0.2	25.1
25–30	9.1	4.3	3.1	4.0	3.6	0.2	24.3
30–50	10.5	4.7	3.0	3.5	2.6	0.2	24.4
50–100	14.1	5.6	2.8	2.4	1.3	0.1	26.4
100–500	18.0	7.4	2.4	1.7	0.7	0.1	30.3
500–1,000	17.7	9.0	1.7	1.4	0.4	0.2	30.3
1,000 and over	16.6	9.8	0.8	1.3	0.3	0.2	29.0
All classesᵇ	8.4	4.4	3.4	5.0	4.4	0.3	25.9

Source: Computed from the 1966 MERGE data file. For an explanation of the incidence variants, see Table 3-1.
Note: Variant 1c is the most progressive and 3b the least progressive set of incidence assumptions examined in this study.
ᵃ Less than 0.05 percent.
ᵇ Includes negative incomes not shown separately.

be shifted to the consumer through higher prices. Thus the effective payroll tax rate at the two ends of the distribution is increased as compared with Variant 1c.

Personal property taxes and motor vehicle licenses are regressive at the lower end of the income scale and proportional or slightly progressive in the higher classes. The effect of these taxes on relative tax burdens is small because they amount to no more than 0.4 percent of income throughout the income scale.

The crucial factors in determining the degree of progressivity in the tax system as a whole are the assumptions made with respect to the incidence of the *corporation income tax* and the *property tax*. If it is assumed that these are taxes on corporate stockholders and owners of property (Variant 1c), they are highly progressive. The corporation income tax rises from about 2 percent of income at the bottom of the income scale to almost 26 percent at the top; the property tax rises from about 2.5 percent to 10 percent.[18] Assuming that half of the corporation income tax is a tax on consumption and that the property taxes on improvements are taxes on shelter and consumption (Variant 3b), progressivity virtually disappears. Since the ratio of total consumption and housing expenditures to annual income falls as incomes rise, the burden of the corporation income tax under Variant 3b is U-shaped, while the property tax is regressive throughout the income scale. Together these two taxes amount to only 10.6 percent of income for families with incomes above $1,000,000 under Variant 3b, as compared with a total of 35.8 percent under 1c.

When the effective rates of the various taxes are examined by population deciles (see Table 4-9), the picture changes only in details. Since all families with incomes of about $20,000 and over are grouped in the top income decile, some of the significant differences in the effective tax rates at the top of the income scale disappear. For example, when families are grouped by absolute income, as in Table 4-8, the individual income tax appears progressive throughout the income scale, even though it is slightly regressive at the very highest income level. Similarly, while the general pattern of rates

---

[18] The slight decline in the effective rates of these taxes at the $5,000 income level reflects the fact that low-income, aged persons receive relatively large proportions of their income from property in the form of interest and dividends and, in the case of homeowners, imputed rent.

TABLE 4-9. Effective Rates of Federal, State, and Local Taxes, by Type of Tax, Variants 1c and 3b, by Population Decile, 1966

Percent

Population decile	Indi- vidual income tax	Corpo- ration income tax	Property tax	Sales and excise taxes	Payroll taxes	Personal property and motor vehicle taxes	Total taxes
			Variant 1c				
First[a]	1.1	1.7	2.1	8.9	2.6	0.4	16.8
Second	2.3	2.1	2.6	7.8	3.8	0.4	18.9
Third	4.0	2.2	2.6	7.1	5.4	0.4	21.7
Fourth	5.4	1.9	2.1	6.7	6.1	0.4	22.6
Fifth	6.3	1.7	1.8	6.4	6.3	0.3	22.8
Sixth	7.0	1.5	1.6	6.1	6.2	0.3	22.7
Seventh	7.5	1.6	1.7	5.7	5.8	0.3	22.7
Eighth	8.3	1.8	1.8	5.5	5.4	0.3	23.1
Ninth	8.8	2.2	2.2	5.0	4.8	0.3	23.3
Tenth	11.4	8.1	5.1	3.2	2.2	0.2	30.1
All deciles[b]	8.5	3.9	3.0	5.1	4.4	0.3	25.2
			Variant 3b				
First[a]	1.2	6.1	6.4	8.9	4.5	0.4	27.5
Second	2.0	5.4	5.1	7.5	4.5	0.4	24.8
Third	3.9	5.0	4.6	6.8	5.4	0.4	26.0
Fourth	5.1	4.4	3.8	6.5	5.7	0.3	25.9
Fifth	6.0	4.1	3.3	6.2	5.8	0.3	25.8
Sixth	6.7	3.9	3.2	5.9	5.6	0.3	25.6
Seventh	7.3	3.7	3.2	5.6	5.4	0.3	25.5
Eighth	8.0	3.7	3.2	5.3	5.0	0.3	25.5
Ninth	8.4	3.9	3.2	4.9	4.5	0.3	25.1
Tenth	11.9	5.2	2.9	3.3	2.5	0.2	25.9
All deciles[b]	8.4	4.4	3.4	5.0	4.4	0.3	25.9

Source: Computed from the 1966 MERGE data file. For an explanation of the incidence variants, see Table 3-1.
Note: Variant 1c is the most progressive and 3b the least progressive set of incidence assumptions examined in this study.
  a. Includes only units in the sixth to tenth percentiles.
  b. Includes negative incomes not shown separately.

found for other taxes does not change when families are classified by income decile, extreme values at both ends of the income scale are moderated. Thus the top corporation tax rate in Table 4-9 (under 1c) is only 8.1 percent, compared with 25.7 percent in Table 4-8. The effective payroll tax rates move in the opposite direction in the two tables: in Table 4-8, the average effective rate in the top income class is less than 1.0 percent; in Table 4-9, the rate in the highest decile is 2.2 percent.

The Burdens of Federal versus State-Local Taxes

In 1966 almost 90 percent of federal revenue was obtained from the individual income, corporation income, and payroll taxes. The states and localities relied primarily on general sales and excise taxes and the property tax. These differences in revenue sources created substantial differences in relative tax burdens at the federal and the state-local levels.

Effective tax rates for federal and state-local taxes—again shown only for the most and least progressive incidence variants, 1c and 3b—are given in Table 4-10. Federal taxes are progressive under both variants, but they are much more progressive with the 1c than with the 3b assumptions. Under 1c, the effective tax rates at the top of the

TABLE 4-10. Effective Rates of Federal and State-Local Taxes, Variants 1c and 3b, by Adjusted Family Income Class, 1966

Income classes in thousands of dollars; tax rates in percent

Adjusted family income	Variant 1c			Variant 3b		
	Federal	State-local	Total	Federal	State-local	Total
0–3	8.8	9.8	18.7	14.1	14.0	28.1
3–5	11.9	8.5	20.4	14.6	10.6	25.3
5–10	15.4	7.2	22.6	17.0	8.9	25.9
10–15	16.3	6.5	22.8	17.5	8.0	25.5
15–20	16.7	6.5	23.2	17.7	7.6	25.3
20–25	17.1	6.9	24.0	17.8	7.4	25.1
25–30	17.4	7.7	25.1	17.2	7.1	24.3
30–50	18.2	8.2	26.4	17.7	6.7	24.4
50–100	21.8	9.7	31.5	20.1	6.3	26.4
100–500	30.0	11.9	41.8	24.4	6.0	30.3
500–1,000	34.6	13.3	48.0	25.2	5.1	30.3
1,000 and over	35.5	13.8	49.3	24.8	4.2	29.0
All classes[a]	17.6	7.6	25.2	17.9	8.0	25.9

Source: Computed from the 1966 MERGE data file. For an explanation of the incidence variants, see Table 3-1. Details may not add to totals because of rounding.
   Note: Variant 1c is the most progressive and 3b the least progressive set of incidence assumptions examined in this study.
   [a] Includes negative incomes not shown separately.

income scale are about four times as high as the rate at the lowest income level; under 3b, the effective rate at the top is less than twice that at the bottom of the income scale. Again, these differences reflect different assumptions as to the incidence of the corporation income tax under the two variants. Variant 3b allocates a substantial portion of this tax to low- and middle-income families. As a result, the federal tax burden is increased by over 5 percentage points for those with incomes under $3,000 and by nearly 3 percentage points for those at the $3,000–$5,000 income level. Correspondingly, the federal tax burden at the top of the income scale is reduced by almost 11 percentage points.

Although state-local taxes are generally believed to be regressive, this conclusion holds only under a specific set of incidence assumptions. Under Variant 3b, which allocates property taxes on improvements on the basis of outlays for shelter and consumption in general, effective state and local tax rates start at 14 percent for families at the bottom of the income scale and decline steadily as income rises. On these assumptions, state-local taxes for those at the top of the income scale amount to only 4 percent of income.

The picture changes dramatically when property taxes on improvements are allocated on the basis of property ownership. Under Variant 1c, average effective state-local tax rates have a U-shaped pattern, which begins at almost 10 percent for families with incomes under $3,000, declines to 6.5 percent for incomes between $10,000 and $20,000, and then rises to almost 14 percent for those with incomes of $1 million or more.

As was the case earlier, when families are arrayed by relative rather than absolute income levels, the average effective tax rates at the high end of the income scale are moderated considerably. Thus in Table 4-11, effective federal rates under Variant 1c rise to only 21.1 percent in the top decile, compared with 35.5 percent for the highest income class in Table 4-10. The highest state-local tax rate in the top decile (shown in Table 4-11) is 9.0 percent, a considerable drop from the 13.8 percent rate shown in Table 4-10 for those with incomes of $1 million or more. Effective tax rates at the bottom of the income distribution are roughly the same whether the units are classified by absolute or by relative incomes.

The general shape of effective tax rates by income levels is not changed if families are classified by relative, rather than by absolute

Who Bears the Tax Burden?

TABLE 4-11. Effective Rates of Federal and State-Local Taxes, Variants 1c and 3b, by Population Decile, 1966

Percent

Population decile	Variant 1c			Variant 3b		
	Federal	State-local	Total	Federal	State-local	Total
First[a]	7.8	9.1	16.8	13.8	13.7	27.5
Second	10.2	8.6	18.9	13.7	11.1	24.8
Third	13.5	8.2	21.7	15.8	10.2	26.0
Fourth	15.1	7.5	22.6	16.8	9.1	25.9
Fifth	15.9	6.9	22.8	17.4	8.4	25.8
Sixth	16.1	6.6	22.7	17.4	8.2	25.6
Seventh	16.2	6.5	22.7	17.5	8.0	25.5
Eighth	16.6	6.5	23.1	17.7	7.9	25.5
Ninth	16.7	6.6	23.3	17.6	7.5	25.1
Tenth	21.1	9.0	30.1	19.2	6.6	25.9
All deciles[b]	17.6	7.6	25.2	17.9	8.0	25.9

Source: Computed from the 1966 MERGE data file. For an explanation of the incidence variants, see Table 3-1.
Details may not add to totals because of rounding.
Note: Variant 1c is the most progressive and 3b the least progressive set of incidence assumptions examined in this study.
[a] Includes only units in the sixth to tenth percentiles.
[b] Includes negative incomes not shown separately.

income levels. Federal tax rates are progressive throughout the income distribution under Variants 1c and 3b, while state-local tax rates retain their regressive pattern under Variant 3b and their U-shaped pattern under 1c.

Summary

Regardless of the incidence assumptions, the tax system is virtually proportional for the vast majority of families in the United States. Under the most progressive set of assumptions examined in this study (Variant 1c), taxes reduce income inequality by less than 5 percent; under the least progressive assumptions (3b), income inequality is reduced by only about 0.25 percent.

Effective tax rates are high at both the bottom and the top of the income scale. The high rates for those in the lowest income classes are probably not indicative of their tax burdens over longer periods, because in these classes there is a heavy concentration of retired persons, as well as of individuals whose incomes are low temporarily. The very rich pay high taxes because a substantial portion of their income comes from property. If it is assumed that the corporation income and property taxes are taxes on income from capital, the tax burden of families with incomes of $1,000,000 or more approaches 50 percent, or roughly double the rates paid by most families. If these taxes are assumed to be shifted in whole or in part to consumers, the tax burden at the highest income level is only about 30 percent, or some 5 percentage points more than the effective rates paid by most families.

The crucial nature of the incidence assumptions in evaluating the progressivity of a tax system is evident when effective rates of federal and state-local taxes are compared. State-local taxes are generally believed to be regressive, but this depends on the assumed incidence of the property tax. If the property tax is regarded as a tax on owners of capital, state-local tax burdens have a U-shaped pattern, with the lightest burdens in the $10,000–$25,000 income range. Federal taxes are progressive throughout the income scale (except for the lowest income classes) under all the incidence assumptions used in this study.

CHAPTER FIVE

Variations in Tax Burdens among Population Subgroups

THE STRUCTURAL FEATURES of the tax system affect different types of income and spending differently. As a consequence, relative tax burdens depend not only on the amount of income a family receives, but also on the sources of the income and the way in which it is spent. They also depend on whether a family owns assets or borrows money and, in particular, whether it owns a house that is mortgaged. All of these factors work to produce very different relative tax burdens—even among families with the same income—whatever the true incidence of taxation may be.

This chapter summarizes the major differences in relative tax burdens on the basis of the alternative sets of incidence assumptions used in this study. (See Table 3-1 above.) It begins by discussing the variability of overall effective tax rates in different parts of the income scale. Then it compares the tax burdens of various demographic and economic groups in the population: the aged and the nonaged, homeowners and renters, single persons and families, and urban and farm families. These are followed by two sets of calculations that show the average tax burdens on families with different major sources of income, and on the total income from labor and from capital. Finally, the results of a statistical analysis made to identify the characteristics of family units that appear to bear especially heavy burdens and of those that enjoy relatively favorable tax treatment are reported.

Variations by and within Deciles

Average effective tax rates and their variability under incidence Variants 1c and 3b—the most and the least progressive sets of assumptions used in this study—are given in Table 5-1 for family units arranged by relative family income level. The statistics, which are calculated for each one-tenth (or decile) of the income distribution, include two measures of central tendency—the mean and the median —and two measures of variability—the standard deviation and the quartile deviation. The statistics for the first decile are calculated only for families in the top half (that is, those between the sixth and tenth population percentiles) because annual incomes in the first five per-

TABLE 5-1. Mean and Median Effective Federal, State, and Local Tax Rates and Measures of Variability of Tax Rates under Incidence Variants 1c and 3b, by Population Decile, 1966

Percent

Population decile	Variant 1c				Variant 3b			
	Mean	Standard deviation[a]	Median	Quartile deviation[a]	Mean	Standard deviation[a]	Median	Quartile deviation[a]
First[b]	16.8	30.1	15.3	6.1	27.6	35.9	23.0	6.6
Second	18.6	14.6	17.8	5.3	24.8	16.3	23.6	4.9
Third	21.6	19.6	21.3	4.1	26.0	12.6	25.0	4.2
Fourth	22.6	8.8	22.1	3.8	25.9	10.5	25.2	3.7
Fifth	22.8	6.5	22.6	3.2	25.8	7.3	25.4	3.2
Sixth	22.7	5.5	22.6	2.8	25.6	5.8	25.6	2.6
Seventh	22.7	6.6	22.4	2.7	25.5	5.5	25.3	2.4
Eighth	23.1	5.9	22.7	2.5	25.5	5.2	25.4	2.2
Ninth	23.2	5.4	22.9	2.4	25.1	4.9	25.1	2.2
Tenth	26.2	10.2	24.5	3.9	25.0	8.6	24.6	2.5

Source: Computed from the 1966 MERGE data file. For an explanation of the incidence variants, see Table 3-1
Note: Variant 1c is the most progressive and 3b the least progressive set of incidence assumptions used in this study.
a. See text for the definition of the standard deviation and the quartile deviation.
b. Includes only units in the sixth to tenth percentiles.

centiles are not representative of the incomes of such units over a longer period.[1]

The mean and median effective rates confirm what is already known about Variants 1c and 3b from the discussion in Chapter 4. The effective rates for total taxes are much more progressive under Variant 1c assumptions than under 3b asssmptions. In every decile and under both variants, the mean or average effective rate is higher than the median (except in two cases where they are equal), because effective rates have a lower limit (zero) and thus there is less room for variation below the median than above. The differences between the mean and the median effective rates are largest in the lowest and the highest deciles under Variant 1c and in the lowest decile under 3b.

The quartile deviation and the standard deviation shed further light on the degree of variability of effective rates. The quartile deviation measures the range above and below the median within which one-half of the family units are concentrated. The standard deviation is a similar measure of dispersion around the mean.[2] Both measures show the largest amount of variability at the low end of the income scale. For example, based on the quartile deviation, under Variant 1c half of the family units pay tax at effective rates between 9.2 and 21.4 percent in the lowest decile, between 19.4 and 25.8 percent in the fifth decile, and between 20.6 and 28.4 percent in the top decile. Under Variant 3b the interquartile ranges are 16.4 to 29.6 percent in the first decile, 22.2 to 28.6 percent in the fifth decile, and 22.1 to 27.1 percent in the top decile.

To help explain the variability of effective rates, the contribution of each tax to the total variance is shown in Table 5-2 for each decile.[3] Under both sets of incidence assumptions, total variance is highest in

---

[1] See the discussion of this subject in Chapter 4.

[2] The standard deviation is the square root of the average of the squared deviation from the distribution mean of each observation in the distribution. If a distribution is normal, about two-thirds of the observations lie in a range that begins one standard deviation below the mean and extends to one standard deviation above the mean.

[3] The variance is the average of the squared deviations above and below the mean; thus, it is equal to the square of the standard deviation. It can be shown mathematically that the total variance is equal to the sum of the variances of effective rates of each tax plus the net covariance among all the taxes. As Table 5-2 shows, the net covariance is positive in the lowest deciles and then becomes negative at higher income levels.

TABLE 5-2. Total Variance[a] in Tax Rates Accounted for by the Major Federal, State, and Local Taxes under Incidence Variants 1c and 3b, by Population Decile, 1966

Percent

Population decile	Individual income tax	Corpo- ration income tax	Property tax	Sales and excise taxes	Payroll taxes	Personal property and motor vehicle taxes	Other[b]	Total taxes
				Variant 1c				
First[c]	662.6	25.8	19.5	43.2	21.3	0.7	131.7	904.8
Second	90.0	15.2	23.8	19.7	20.1	0.4	45.5	214.5
Third	309.4	15.2	18.0	9.8	15.5	0.4	15.2	383.5
Fourth	27.7	25.0	16.1	6.8	11.5	0.1	−9.3	77.9
Fifth	24.6	11.0	8.5	4.6	9.4	0.1	−16.1	42.1
Sixth	18.1	8.8	5.7	3.1	7.0	0.1	−12.2	30.6
Seventh	30.9	8.5	6.4	2.7	6.5	0.2	−10.9	44.2
Eighth	23.0	9.0	4.7	2.2	5.7	0.1	−10.0	34.6
Ninth	20.1	10.4	5.1	1.8	5.4	0.1	−14.0	28.9
Tenth	76.4	39.8	11.4	1.6	6.4	d	−31.6	104.0
				Variant 3b				
First[c]	215.0	25.8	392.8	48.3	11.9	0.6	597.0	1,291.5
Second	149.3	9.0	19.6	18.5	7.9	0.3	60.4	265.0
Third	59.7	7.7	24.6	9.4	7.2	0.4	49.3	158.2
Fourth	52.9	5.6	23.9	6.1	5.4	0.2	17.0	111.1
Fifth	28.6	4.2	5.6	4.4	4.3	0.1	6.0	53.2
Sixth	20.2	3.6	5.8	2.8	3.3	0.1	−2.3	33.4
Seventh	20.5	2.5	3.6	2.4	2.8	0.1	−1.3	30.6
Eighth	19.5	2.3	3.0	1.9	2.5	0.1	−2.5	26.8
Ninth	18.7	3.0	3.2	1.6	2.4	0.1	−4.8	24.1
Tenth	78.2	5.3	4.2	1.5	3.3	0.1	−18.2	74.4

Source: Computed from the 1966 MERGE data file. For an explanation of the incidence variants, see Table 3-1.
Details may not add to totals because of rounding.
Note: Variant 1c is the most progressive and Variant 3b the least progressive set of incidence assumptions used in this study.
[a] Variance is equal to the average sum of squared deviations above and below the mean.
[b] Amount due to net interaction among all taxes.
[c] Includes only units in the sixth to tenth percentiles.
[d] Less than 0.05 percent.

the first few deciles and then drops steadily through the ninth decile of the income distribution. Under each variant, the total variance in effective rates is lowest in the ninth decile—a range that includes absolute income levels of about $15,000 to $20,000—and it then increases in the highest decile.

In virtually all deciles, the individual income tax accounts for a major share of the total variance. This occurs because the individual income tax is designed to differentiate among family units with similar incomes on the basis of particular family characteristics (for example, marital status of the family head, family size, homeownership, contributions, and so on). In addition, income from some sources is taxed at preferential rates (or not at all), while that from other sources is taxed in full. The result is that there is wide variation in individual income tax liabilities among family units within the same decile. Thus under Variant 1c the individual income tax accounts for 73 percent of the total variance in effective tax rates in both the bottom and the top decile. Under 3b the individual income tax accounts for only 17 percent of the total variance in the bottom decile and 105 percent in the top decile.[4]

The variance of corporation income and property tax rates is significantly higher in the upper half of the income distribution under Variant 1c than under 3b because these taxes are allocated on the basis of income from capital. Such income is received by a minority of family units, and as a result the allocation of these taxes is far from uniform. In most deciles the variance of the corporation income and property taxes under 3b is much smaller than under 1c because a substantial proportion of these taxes is allocated on the basis of total consumption expenditures or expenditures for housing, which do not vary as much as does income from property at any particular income level.[5]

The variance of payroll tax rates is lower under Variant 3b than under 1c because half of these taxes are allocated on the basis of consumption under 3b. As has been noted, the ratio of consumption expenditures to income does not vary greatly. The uniformity of consumption ratios also explains why the variance in sales and excise tax rates is roughly the same under the two sets of assumptions.

[4] The contribution of the variance of effective rates of a single tax may exceed the total variance if the net covariation is negative, which is the case in the top decile under Variant 3b assumptions.

[5] Consumption was attributed to each family unit on the basis of averages for particular income classes and demographic groups. (See Appendix B.) As a result, the variability under Variant 3b and the other variants that treat the corporation income and property taxes as taxes on consumption or housing is understated somewhat in these calculations.

Variations among Demographic and Economic Groups

The MERGE file contains a number of identifying characteristics for each family unit that are associated with significant variations in tax burdens. The characteristics that are of particular interest for tax analysis are age of family head, homeownership, place of residence, marital status, and family size. Effective rates under Variants 1c and 3b for family units classified on the basis of these characteristics are given for each major tax in Table 5-3 and in the aggregate by population deciles in Tables 5-4 and 5-5.

Aged and Nonaged

In 1966, 19 percent of all family units were headed by a person aged sixty-five or over. These families paid lower individual income, consumption, and payroll taxes than did families headed by persons under sixty-five years of age, but they paid higher corporation income and property taxes.

The aged pay lower individual income taxes partly because their incomes are lower and partly because they are given special treatment (mainly through extra personal exemptions) under the federal and most of the state income taxes. They pay lower payroll taxes because most of them are retired and lower consumption taxes because they generally spend relatively less for consumption of highly taxed commodities than do the nonaged.[6] On the other hand, the aged pay higher corporation income and property taxes because they own more property and consume more shelter.[7]

The relative tax burdens of families headed by aged and nonaged

---

[6] According to the MERGE file, under Variant 1c, consumption of such highly taxed commodities as liquor, tobacco, gasoline, and automobiles averaged 4.5 percent of adjusted family income for families headed by a person sixty-five years of age or over and 7.8 percent for families headed by someone under sixty-five. The percentages were roughly the same under the other incidence variants.

[7] As of the end of 1962, net worth averaged $30,124 for families headed by a person aged sixty-five or over and $19,984 for all families. (Dorothy S. Projector, *Survey of Changes in Family Finances* [Board of Governors of the Federal Reserve System, 1968], p. 316.) At the same time, 61 percent of families headed by an aged person owned their homes, as compared with 57 percent for all families. (Dorothy S. Projector and Gertrude S. Weiss, *Survey of Financial Characteristics of Consumers* [Board of Governors of the Federal Reserve System, 1966], pp. 110–11.)

TABLE 5-3. Effective Federal, State, and Local Tax Rates for Various Demographic and Economic Groups under Incidence Variants 1c and 3b, 1966

Percent

Group and variant	Individual income tax	Corpo- ration income tax	Property tax	Sales and excise taxes	Payroll taxes	Personal property and motor vehicle taxes	Total taxes
Nonaged							
Variant 1c	8.7	3.2	2.5	5.2	4.9	0.3	24.8
Variant 3b	8.6	4.1	3.2	5.1	4.6	0.3	25.9
Aged							
Variant 1c	6.9	8.2	5.9	4.5	1.9	0.2	27.6
Variant 3b	7.2	6.6	4.4	4.7	2.8	0.2	25.9
Homeowners							
Variant 1c	8.4	4.4	3.4	4.7	4.0	0.3	25.2
Variant 3b	8.3	4.6	3.6	4.7	4.0	0.3	25.6
Renters							
Variant 1c	8.7	2.7	1.9	6.1	5.6	0.2	25.3
Variant 3b	8.5	4.0	2.8	6.0	5.3	0.2	26.9
Urban							
Variant 1c	9.0	3.8	2.7	5.0	4.6	0.3	25.4
Variant 3b	9.0	4.2	3.1	5.0	4.5	0.3	26.0
Rural-farm							
Variant 1c	6.0	4.6	4.3	5.4	3.7	0.3	24.3
Variant 3b	6.0	5.5	4.6	5.3	3.8	0.3	25.5
Single persons							
Variant 1c	11.1	6.5	3.7	5.7	4.3	0.2	31.6
Variant 3b	11.5	5.0	3.0	5.9	4.6	0.2	30.2
Married couples, no children							
Variant 1c	9.0	5.9	4.3	4.7	3.7	0.3	27.9
Variant 3b	9.2	5.2	3.6	4.8	3.8	0.3	26.8
Married couples, two children							
Variant 1c	8.7	2.7	2.2	5.0	4.8	0.3	23.8
Variant 3b	8.5	3.8	3.1	4.9	4.6	0.3	25.2

Source: Computed from the 1966 MERGE data file. For an explanation of the incidence variants, see Table 3-1.
Note: Variant 1c is the most progressive and 3b the least progressive set of incidence assumptions used in this study.

TABLE 5-4. Effective Federal, State, and Local Tax Rates under Incidence Variant 1c for Population Subgroups, by Population Decile, 1966

Percent

Population decile	All families	Age of family head		Homeowners	Renters	Urban	Rural-farm	Single persons	Married couples	
		Under 65	65 and over						No children	Two children
First[a]	16.8	19.7	14.3	19.6	15.5	16.0	19.0	19.0	17.4	19.7
Second	18.9	21.1	15.9	18.7	19.0	18.6	19.6	23.6	17.9	20.5
Third	21.7	22.5	19.6	21.0	22.4	21.6	22.1	27.0	20.8	20.8
Fourth	22.6	22.7	21.8	22.0	23.1	22.8	21.9	28.0	23.3	20.9
Fifth	22.8	22.8	23.3	22.3	23.5	22.8	23.1	28.0	24.5	21.4
Sixth	22.7	22.5	23.9	22.1	23.6	22.7	22.7	28.0	24.5	21.5
Seventh	22.7	22.5	24.6	22.3	23.6	22.8	22.4	26.6	24.8	21.4
Eighth	23.1	22.9	26.1	22.6	24.9	23.2	22.5	30.3	25.4	21.9
Ninth	23.3	23.0	25.9	23.0	24.5	23.4	22.3	30.1	25.8	22.3
Tenth	30.1	28.9	35.1	29.8	31.8	30.8	27.3	42.9	33.7	27.4
All deciles[b]	25.2	24.8	27.6	25.2	25.3	25.4	24.3	31.6	27.9	23.8

Source: Computed from the 1966 MERGE data file. For an explanation of the incidence variant, see Table 3-1.
[a] Includes only units in the sixth to tenth percentiles.
[b] Includes negative incomes not shown separately.

persons depend on the assumptions made as to the incidence of the corporation income and property taxes. If it is assumed that these taxes are borne by owners of capital (Variant 1c), the aged pay 2.5 times as much corporation income and property taxes relative to their incomes as do the nonaged (14.1 percent as compared with 5.7 percent). In the lower income groups, this is more than enough to offset the relatively lower individual income, payroll, and consumption tax rates of the aged, but not in the top 60 percent of income recipients. (See Table 5-4.) Overall, under Variant 1c, the aged pay 27.6 percent of their income in taxes, while the nonaged pay 24.8 percent.

If the corporation income and property taxes are assumed to be passed on at least in part to consumers (Variant 3b), relative to income the aged pay about 1.5 times as much of these taxes as do the nonaged (11.0 percent, compared with 7.3 percent). In the aggregate, this is just enough to offset the lower burdens imposed by the other taxes, so that aged and nonaged families pay an average of 25.9 percent of their incomes in taxes. However, in the lowest 90 percent of the income distribution, aged families pay lower taxes than do nonaged families; in the top 10 percent, aged families pay higher taxes because of the importance of property taxes and the corporation income tax. (See Table 5-5.)

Homeowners and Renters

Almost 60 percent of all families in the United States owned their own homes in 1966; the other 40 percent rented. Under both Variants 1c and 3b, families who live in their own homes pay lower individual income taxes than do those who rent because the net imputed rental income from dwellings is excluded from taxable income while mortgage interest and property tax payments are deductible; homeowners also pay lower payroll and consumption taxes than do renters. However, they pay higher corporation income and property taxes because they own more property. On balance, the total tax burden of homeowners is lower than that of renters under both variants—although the difference under 1c is small.[8] The same general pattern of burdens

---

[8] The difference is small for all family units under Variant 1c because the totals include units with negative incomes. These units have large amounts of property relative to income and are therefore allocated relatively large amounts of corporation income and property taxes under Variant 1c. As a result, the total tax burdens of all homeowners as a group are not very different from the burdens of all renters, even though they are much lower in every population decile but the first.

TABLE 5-5. Effective Federal, State, and Local Tax Rates under Incidence Variant 3b for Population Subgroups, by Population Decile, 1966

Percent

| Population decile | All families | Age of family head | | Homeowners | Renters | Urban residents | Rural-farm residents | Single persons | Married couples | |
		Under 65	65 and over						No children	Two children
First[a]	27.5	29.1	26.1	28.7	26.9	26.3	30.3	27.8	29.4	38.8
Second	24.8	26.0	23.4	25.7	24.1	24.7	25.3	27.4	24.6	25.8
Third	26.0	26.7	24.5	25.9	26.2	25.9	26.5	30.1	25.4	25.6
Fourth	25.9	26.2	24.1	25.4	26.3	25.9	25.9	30.7	26.3	24.7
Fifth	25.8	26.0	24.6	25.4	26.3	25.7	26.1	30.3	26.7	24.9
Sixth	25.6	25.8	24.1	25.3	26.1	25.6	25.5	29.7	26.4	25.1
Seventh	25.5	25.5	25.3	25.2	26.2	25.6	25.1	29.1	26.6	24.6
Eighth	25.5	25.6	25.1	25.2	26.6	25.6	25.2	31.2	27.1	24.7
Ninth	25.1	25.2	24.7	25.0	25.8	25.3	23.9	29.9	26.7	24.3
Tenth	25.9	25.5	27.5	25.9	26.0	26.5	23.3	29.3	26.5	25.5
All deciles[b]	25.9	25.9	25.9	25.6	26.9	26.0	25.5	30.2	26.8	25.2

Source: Computed from the 1966 MERGE data file. For an explanation of the incidence variant, see Table 3-1.
a. Includes only units in the sixth to tenth percentiles.
b. Includes negative incomes not shown separately.

is found in the effective tax rates of the two groups at different income levels. (See Tables 5-4 and 5-5.) Except for units in the lowest income deciles, the homeowners' lower individual income, payroll, and consumption taxes more than offset the higher corporation income and property taxes.

Urban and Rural Residents

About 78 percent of all families lived in urban communities in 1966, and the remaining 22 percent lived in rural-farm areas. The total taxes paid by the urban residents are somewhat higher than the taxes paid by the rural group, but the difference is not large (25.4 percent for urban residents as against 24.3 percent for rural residents under Variant 1c; and 26.0 percent versus 25.5 percent under 3b). However, there are substantial differences in the burdens imposed by particular taxes on the two groups. Urban residents pay about 50 percent higher individual income taxes than do residents of rural areas, but they bear relatively lower corporation income and property taxes. The higher individual income taxes of the urban group reflect the fact that they have higher incomes and also are subject to higher effective individual income tax rates.[9] Farm families pay higher corporation and property taxes than do urban families because they own more property relative to income. As in the case of homeowners and renters, rural-farm families pay higher total taxes than do urban residents in the lower part of the income distribution and lower taxes in the upper part.

Family Size and Marital Status

In 1966, single persons constituted about 10 percent of all family units, married couples with no children 21 percent, families with children 49 percent, and all other family units 20 percent.[10] Regardless of the incidence assumptions, the smaller the size of the family, the higher the taxes they paid. For example, under Variant 1c, single persons paid 31.6 percent of their income in taxes, married couples

[9] Farmers receive favorable treatment under the federal income tax in a number of respects. For example, they are subject to capital gains rates on profits from the sale of breeding livestock and are allowed to deduct numerous capital expenditures as current expense.

[10] The other units were families of two or more related persons, headed by an unmarried person, and families with only one spouse present.

with no children paid 27.9 percent, and married couples with two children paid 23.8 percent. The corresponding rates for Variant 3b were 30.2 percent, 26.8 percent, and 25.2 percent, respectively. These differences are due in large measure to the greater weight of the individual income tax on smaller families as a result of fewer personal exemptions and, in the case of single persons, the denial of any income-splitting advantages.[11] Under Variant 1c, which allocates the corporation income tax to families on the basis of ownership of corporate stock and other capital, the corporation tax burden is also inversely related to family size. This probably reflects the concentration among small family units of the aged, who tend to own more wealth than do younger people.[12] The differences in the burdens of other taxes do not appear to be systematically related to family size.

The pattern of relative tax burdens by family size shown by the aggregate data generally holds for different parts of the income distribution. In most deciles, effective rates of tax decline as family size increases. (See Tables 5-4 and 5-5.) Exceptions to this pattern occur in the first few deciles, where the tax value of the personal income tax exemptions and of income splitting is relatively small.

Variations by Source of Income

It is well known that relative tax burdens depend heavily on the sources from which income is derived. In this section, the effect of different income sources is examined in two ways. First, effective tax rates are calculated for families, classified by their largest source of income. Second, all taxes are allocated among labor, capital, and consumption; the effective rates of tax on labor income, income from capital, and consumption are then compared.

Taxes on Families by Major Source of Income

In 1966 the largest source of income for 70 percent of all families was wages; for 7 percent of all families it was farm or nonfarm business income; for 10 percent it was income from property; and for

[11] Effective in 1970, the federal income tax rates of single persons were lowered in order to reduce the relative advantages of married couples under income splitting. Thus it is likely that the differential in tax burden of single persons and married couples has been narrowed since 1966.

[12] See page 71, note 7.

TABLE 5-6. Effective Rates of Federal, State, and Local Taxes, by Type of Tax, Variants 1c and 3b, Families Classified by Major Source of Income, 1966

Percent

Major source of income	Individual income tax	Corpo-ration income tax	Property tax	Sales and excise taxes	Payroll taxes	Personal property and motor vehicle taxes	Total taxes
			Variant 1c				
Wages[a]	8.9	1.3	1.3	5.6	5.8	0.3	23.2
Business[b]	10.0	4.0	4.8	4.6	2.0	0.2	25.7
Property[c]	7.3	15.0	9.2	3.0	0.7	0.2	35.4
Transfer[d]	0.4	1.8	2.3	7.7	0.8	0.3	13.2
			Variant 3b				
Wages[a]	8.6	3.4	2.9	5.4	5.2	0.3	25.7
Business[b]	9.9	5.5	4.6	4.5	3.0	0.2	27.7
Property[c]	8.2	8.7	4.6	3.4	1.5	0.2	26.7
Transfer[d]	0.4	5.4	5.1	7.5	2.8	0.3	21.5

Source: Computed from the 1966 MERGE data file. For an explanation of the incidence variants, see Table 3-1.
Note: Variant 1c is the most progressive and Variant 3b the least progressive set of incidence assumptions used in this study.
[a] The sum of wages, salaries, and wage supplements.
[b] The sum of farm and nonfarm business income.
[c] The sum of interest, corporation profits before tax, rents, royalties, and other gains on capital assets.
[d] The sum of social security benefits, unemployment insurance and workmen's compensation, and public assistance.

another 12 percent, transfer payments.[13] As might be expected, families the major portion of whose income came from property or business had the highest tax burdens, while those whose major source was transfer payments had the lowest. The tax burdens of those who relied on wages were lower than the tax burdens of families relying on property income or business income and higher than those of families relying on transfer payments. (See Table 5-6.)

The relative burdens imposed by the major taxes on each group depend heavily on assumptions as to incidence. Under both variants the corporation tax is the heaviest tax for property income recipients,

[13] Families were classified by major source on the basis of the largest *absolute* amount of income. Thus, a family with a larger business loss than it had positive income from wages, property, or transfer payments was classified as receiving its major source of income from business. Families with no major income source were excluded.

and the individual income tax is the heaviest for those with wage or business income. Recipients of transfer payments pay very little individual income tax under Variant 3b but are heavily burdened by the corporation income tax, the property tax, and consumption taxes. Under both sets of assumptions, the payroll tax is either the second or the third largest tax paid by wage-earning families. Under 1c, the burden of the payroll tax on wage-earning families is exceeded only by that of the income tax; under 3b, it is somewhat less than the sales tax burden.

Taxes on Income Sources

The allocation of taxes among sources of income is of particular interest from the standpoint of tax policy. It is frequently alleged that the tax rates on income from various sources are excessive. Yet the total tax burden imposed on income from particular sources has never been calculated on the basis of the correct aggregates, let alone by income class.[14] The data in the MERGE file permit such calculations to be made for the first time.

In these calculations, taxes were allocated to labor income or income from capital in proportion to the amount of such income that is subject to tax. In the case of the individual income tax, the allocation was made on the basis of income reported on federal tax returns. In the case of other taxes, the allocation was made on the basis of the amount of such income in the MERGE data file. Farm income and nonfarm business income were assumed to represent partly a return to labor and partly a return to capital.[15] All taxes were allocated in accordance with the particular assumptions applicable to each incidence variant.

The effective rates of tax on labor income, on income from cap-

----

[14] Harberger has estimated that, in 1967, taxes amounted to more than 50 percent on the net national product generated by capital. (Arnold C. Harberger, "Introduction," in Harberger and Martin J. Bailey [eds.], *The Taxation of Income from Capital* [Brookings Institution, 1969], p. 1.) This estimate was prepared on the basis of the national income accounts concepts, which do not correspond to a comprehensive definition of income. See Chapter 2 for a discussion of the differences between the two concepts.

[15] The return to capital was assumed to be 14 percent of nonfarm business net profit and 29 percent of net farm income. These proportions are based on unpublished estimates by Edward F. Denison.

TABLE 5-7. Effective Federal, State, and Local Tax Rates on Sources and Uses of Income under Different Incidence Variants, 1966

Percent

Incidence variant	Sources of income		Uses of income (consumption)[c]
	Labor[a]	Capital[b]	
1a	17.6	34.1	8.3
1b	17.6	33.8	8.3
1c	17.6	33.0	8.3
2a	17.6	26.3	11.9
2b	16.0	26.3	13.9
3a	19.0	19.9	13.3
3b	16.0	21.0	17.6
3c	17.6	30.7	10.0

Source: Computed from the 1966 MERGE data file. For an explanation of the incidence variants, see Table 3-1. For an explanation of the method used to allocate taxes among sources and uses of income, see page 79.

[a] The sum of wages, salaries, wage supplements, 86 percent of nonfarm business income, and 71 percent of farm income.

[b] The sum of interest, corporation profits before tax, rents, royalties, capital gains, 14 percent of nonfarm business income, and 29 percent of farm income.

[c] The sum of total expenditures on consumption items generally subject to state sales and excise taxes.

ital, and on consumption are shown for each variant in Table 5-7.[16] The taxes on labor income did not differ greatly among the variants, since there were relatively minor differences among the assumptions as to the incidence of the taxes applying to labor income. However, the burden of taxation on income from capital was greatly affected by the assumptions used; it ranged from a low of 19.9 percent under Variant 3a to a high of 34.1 percent under 1a. The lower percentage results if it is assumed that one-quarter of the corporation income tax is a tax on consumption and that the property tax is a tax on shelter and consumption. If it is assumed that both taxes are borne by capital income, the higher percentage results. For the same reasons, the effective tax rate on consumption is roughly the mirror image of the rate on income from capital; the lowest rate is 8.3 percent under Variant 1c, and the highest rate is 17.6 percent under 3b.

The same effective rates of tax are shown in Table 5-8 by deciles.

[16] It will be recalled from the discussion in Chapter 3 that taxes were allocated either to sources of income or to uses of income. This ignores the possibility that a particular tax may impose a burden on both the source and the use of income; however, the burdens that were omitted are probably very small as compared with those that were included.

TABLE 5-8. Effective Federal, State, and Local Tax Rates on Sources and Uses of Income under Incidence Variants 1c and 3b, by Population Decile, 1966

Percent

Population decile	Variant 1c			Variant 3b		
	Income from labor[a]	Income from capital[b]	Con-sumption[c]	Income from labor[a]	Income from capital[b]	Con-sumption[c]
First[d]	11.8	27.3	6.8	10.0	22.0	16.1
Second	13.8	26.0	7.7	11.4	17.2	17.1
Third	15.4	25.8	8.4	13.2	18.1	17.7
Fourth	15.9	26.0	8.5	13.6	17.5	17.8
Fifth	16.5	25.5	8.6	14.3	17.1	17.7
Sixth	16.6	24.7	8.6	14.6	16.8	17.9
Seventh	16.8	25.1	8.5	14.9	17.6	18.0
Eighth	17.1	26.2	8.6	15.3	17.7	18.0
Ninth	17.5	27.1	8.3	15.8	17.8	17.8
Tenth	20.2	38.3	7.9	19.3	23.5	17.0
All deciles[e]	17.6	33.0	8.3	16.0	21.0	17.6

Source: Computed from the 1966 MERGE data file. For an explanation of the incidence variants, see Table 3-1. For an explanation of the method used to allocate taxes among sources and uses of income, see page 79.

Note: Variant 1c is the most progressive and 3b the least progressive set of incidence assumptions used in this study.

[a] The sum of wages, salaries, wage supplements, 86 percent of nonfarm business income, and 71 percent of farm income.

[b] The sum of interest, corporation profits before tax, rents, royalties, capital gains, 14 percent of nonfarm business income, and 29 percent of farm income.

[c] The sum of total expenditures on consumption items generally subject to state sales and excise taxes.

[d] Includes only units in the sixth to the tenth percentiles.

[e] Includes negative incomes not shown separately.

The tax on labor income is progressive throughout the income scale, rising from 11.8 percent in the first decile to 20.2 percent in the top decile under Variant 1c and from 10.0 percent to 19.3 percent under 3b. In contrast, the tax on income from capital is U-shaped under both variants, reflecting the relatively high percentage of income received from property in the lowest and highest income classes. In the top decile, the tax on income from capital is only 23.5 percent under Variant 3b, but it is 38.3 percent under 1c.

Although the ratio of consumption to income falls as income rises, sales and excise taxes tend to be proportional to expenditures on the taxed items. Thus, when consumption taxes are expressed as a percentage of consumption expenditures (as in Table 5-8), they are roughly proportional throughout the income scale.

Summary

It is clear that effective tax rates vary substantially among families for many reasons. In addition to differences that arise because of the particular incidence assumptions used, the most important causes of variation in tax rates are the structural provisions of the individual income tax.

When the effective rates on various subgroups of the population are compared, those with the lowest rates are homeowners, rural-farm residents, families with transfers as their major source of income, and large families. Those with the highest effective rates are renters, urban residents, families whose major source of income is property or business, and single persons. These groups are not mutually exclusive, and some units have low (or high) tax rates because they belong to two or more of the groups. To isolate the effect of the demographic factors on variations in effective tax rates, a statistical analysis was made using a nonlinear, multivariate computer program.[17] This was done separately for factors influencing effective tax rates under Variants 1c and 3b.

The analysis for Variant 1c indicates that families the major portion of whose income is from transfers have the lowest tax rates. Such units are predominantly over age sixty-five and single, and have low incomes. Family units that derive large incomes from property pay the highest effective rates. These units are generally headed by a nonaged person and are homeowners. After taking account of the characteristics mentioned above, place of residence (urban or rural-farm) has no significant effect in explaining differences in effective tax rates. Most of the same variables that are important in explaining differences in tax rates under Variant 1c are also included in the 3b results although they tend to have a different order of importance.

The multivariate analysis of Variant 3b shows no significant difference among those whose major income source is wages, property, or business income, whereas the results for 1c separate those with property as their major income source from those who derive most

---

[17] A description of the program and a more detailed discussion of the results are given in Appendix D.

of their income from wages or business. Under both variants, absolute amount of income is important in explaining differences in effective tax rates only for those at the bottom of the income scale. In general, after account is taken of major income source and marital status, the other demographic factors do not contribute importantly to explaining differences in effective tax rates.

The 1966 MERGE Data File

THIS APPENDIX DESCRIBES the methods used to construct the 1966 MERGE data file and to adjust the income components in the file to the aggregates obtained from the national income accounts.

The MERGE file combines data from two basic sources of information on the incomes of individual family units for calendar year 1966: (1) the U.S. Internal Revenue Service file, which contains information from federal individual income tax returns for 1966; and (2) the 1967 Survey of Economic Opportunity (SEO) data file, which is based on field interviews for a sample of the total population in early 1967. The tax file contains a stratified sample of data from nearly 87,000 individual returns.[1] The Survey of Economic Opportunity—conducted by the U.S. Bureau of the Census for the U.S. Office of Economic Opportunity—is based on interviews with about 30,000 households. It includes income information for 1966 and financial and demographic data as of the date of interview. Although neither of these data files by itself is adequate for estimating the size distribution of income needed for this study, each contains information that, when combined, provides a suitable basis for the estimate.

For several reasons, the SEO was chosen as the basis of the new data file. The SEO population is a stratified representation of the total U.S. population on a family basis.[2] The income information collected in the SEO includes receipts from nontaxable as well as taxable sources and is

---

[1] A detailed description of the file is available upon request from the authors.

[2] The term "family" is used to include families of two or more persons as well as persons living alone.

therefore more comprehensive than it would be if it included only income subject to tax. In addition, the demographic data available for each family are much more comprehensive than the data that could be obtained from tax returns. The major disadvantage of the SEO file is that the income data are known to be seriously understated (especially among higher-income families) and capital gains are not included in the survey income concept. Consequently, information from the 1966 tax file and the 1967 SEO file were combined to create what is called the "MERGE file" in this study.

Creating the File

The 1967 SEO file contains data from a stratified sample of all U.S. families and individuals; the 1966 tax file population consists of a subset of this same population—individuals who filed federal income tax returns for that year. On the basis of income and demographic information reported, it was possible to identify the families in the SEO population that would not have been expected to file an income tax return for 1966. The remaining SEO units represented families who were in the population from which the 1966 tax file sample of returns was drawn. For these families, it was possible to estimate the kind of tax returns filed, using reported SEO information. The actual tax return data were then merged with the information in each SEO family record.

For most families, the MERGE data file record contains all the demographic information and data concerning receipts of nontaxable income from the SEO file, as well as data from a tax return assigned to it from the 1966 tax file. For families not filing returns, the MERGE file includes no tax return information. For a small number of very high-income units (see page 88), the file does not contain any SEO demographic data.

Matching Procedures

The initial step in the matching process was to group the tax units in each file into "equivalence classes," defined by comparable characteristics found in both the SEO file and the tax file. The characteristics used were (1) marital status, (2) whether the head of the tax unit (or his spouse) was 65 years of age or over, (3) the number of exemptions for dependents, and (4) the pattern of income.

Information on the first three was available directly from both the SEO and the tax files. The income pattern variable was constructed as follows: First, each tax unit was classified under one of four major categories of income—wage, business, farm, or property income—based on the unit's largest income source in absolute amount. Thus, if a tax unit reported a business loss of $10,000 and dividend income of $500, it was classified in the business major source category even though the property income (dividends) of $500 was algebraically greater. Second, after the major source of income was determined, each return was classified by minor income sources (within each major-source group). Altogether there were thirty-five possible income categories.

Classification by characteristics (1) through (4) listed above would have resulted in more than a thousand different equivalence classes, many of which would have contained very few sample units or none at all. The number of equivalence classes actually used was reduced to seventy-four by eliminating or combining a large number of previously defined categories.[3]

Since a tax file return with exactly the same amount and pattern of income as reported in the SEO tax unit can be found only rarely, the first matching rule was to establish an acceptable range of major-source income from which a tax return could be selected. This was initially set equal to the major-source income of the SEO tax unit, plus or minus 2 percent of that amount. To ensure that this procedure was not too restrictive for low-income units and not too generous for high-income ones, plus or minus $50 was substituted for the 2 percent criterion for units with incomes of $2,500 or less, and plus or minus $500 for units with incomes of $25,000 or more. Thus, if reported major-source income was $6,000, the 2 percent criterion would establish an acceptable income band ranging between $5,880 and $6,120. For a family with major-source income of $1,000, the band would be $950 to $1,050; at $30,000, the band would be $29,500 to $30,500.

For all tax file returns in the acceptable income range within each equivalence class, a "consistency score" was then computed to take account of hitherto unused information for obtaining a suitable tax return match. For each of the factors entering the consistency score, tax return data from each potential match were compared with information in the SEO family record; and if the items were "consistent" (that is, if both were present or both were absent), the return was given consistency score points. The maximum possible consistency score was 57.[4] Only tax file

---

[3] For a list of the seventy-four categories, see Benjamin A. Okner, "Constructing a New Data Base From Existing Microdata Sets: The 1966 MERGE File," *Annals of Economic and Social Measurement,* Vol. 1 (July 1972).

[4] The six factors used in measuring consistency were: (a) home mortgage interest deduction or property tax deduction on tax return and home ownership or debt (or value of house included in farm value) in SEO—twelve points; (b) interest or

returns in the top 25 percent of the initial group when ranked by consistency score were eligible for matching with an SEO tax unit. An additional constraint was imposed: the minimum consistency score in the top quartile had to equal at least twenty-five points out of the possible fifty-seven. This meant that a tax return had to have almost half the maximum possible consistency score in order to be assigned to an SEO tax unit.

All tax returns that passed the consistency score test and were within the acceptable income range for the SEO tax unit being matched to a tax file unit were eligible for selection and linking. From the eligible returns within the group, the return assigned was randomly selected and the probability of being chosen was proportional to the weight of the return in the tax file.[5]

Almost all the matches were made under the procedure just described. However, there were instances when the initially defined income band contained no tax returns or the consistency scores of returns in the initial range did not meet the minimum of twenty-five. When this occurred, the initial income range was increased by an additional 1 percent in each direction, and the minimum and maximum dollar amount constraints on the size of the income range were increased somewhat.[6] Consistency scores were computed for all new returns in the wider income range, and if a suitable match was found (still using the same criteria as above), the computer program assigned the selected tax return to the proper SEO tax unit and proceeded to the next SEO tax unit.

If no suitable match was found on the second try, the class limits were again expanded (by plus and minus 1 percent each time), and consistency scores were computed for the new tax returns that were included in the enlarged set of eligible returns. The computer program terminated after seven unsuccessful attempts at automatic assignment and then carried out

---

dividend income on tax return and interest or dividend income or ownership of stocks, bonds, or other interest-bearing assets in SEO—eight points; (c) farm income on tax return and farm income or farm assets or debt in SEO—ten points; (d) business income on tax return and business income or business assets or debt in SEO—ten points; (e) rental income or real estate property tax deduction on tax return and rental income or real estate assets or debt in SEO—nine points; (f) capital gains income on tax return and dividends, interest, or other property income in SEO, or no capital gains on tax return and property income in SEO—eight points.

[5] This procedure guarantees random selection since the tax file weights are equal to the inverse of the probability of selection from the total universe of tax returns filed for 1966.

[6] Each time the percentage range was increased, the band was widened by plus and minus $10 and the maximum was increased by plus and minus $125. These changes compensated for the percentage changes in the income range.

what was essentially a hand-matching procedure.[7] In actual operation, the class expansions and hand-matching were rarely needed. Of the 28,643 tax unit matches made, 27,912, or 97 percent, were accomplished using the initial criteria.

Weight Adjustment for High-Income Units

After the matching process was completed, substantial differences were discovered between the frequency and amounts of income reported by high-income SEO families and the totals published by the Internal Revenue Service. This discrepancy was the result primarily of the different methods used in drawing the tax file sample and the sample of SEO households. In the SEO sample, high-income families were generally chosen at a sampling rate of 1/3,000, and the data for each family were therefore multiplied by about 3,000 to obtain population estimates. In the tax file sample, the returns were grouped into thirteen strata, depending primarily on income level. The sampling rates for the strata differed, ranging between 1/4,000 for low-income returns to 1/1 for those with very high incomes. As a result of the different sampling schemes, the SEO file contains data on very few high-income families, each of which has a weight of about 3,000; while the tax file contains thousands of high-income returns, each of which has a very low population weight. Thus, when a tax return was matched with one of the high-income SEO tax units, all the tax data originally associated with a very low tax file weight were multiplied by the much larger SEO family weight. Because of these differences in weights, the estimated aggregate amount of income on the returns was initially greatly overstated.

The problem was resolved by splitting the MERGE file into two parts. For all families with positive incomes of less than $30,000, the SEO and tax return data as derived from the match-merge process were accepted. For all SEO families with incomes of $30,000 or more, or with negative incomes, the original SEO records were deleted and replaced with tax file returns. (The $30,000 income level was chosen for splitting the file since at that point the SEO and tax file weights began to diverge by significant amounts.)

Thus the MERGE file does not contain any SEO data for high-income returns or for those on which reported income was negative. Such returns, which accounted for less than 2 percent of the 70.2 million returns filed

---

[7] After seven attempts to make an automatic assignment, a list of all possible tax returns that might be selected was printed out by the computer. The analyst continued to expand the income range for eligible returns until an acceptable match was found. Only 151 of the 28,643 tax unit matches were completed in this way.

TABLE A-1. Detailed Derivation of Family Income from National Income, 1966

Millions of dollars

Description	Amount
National income (as defined in the national income accounts)	**620,585**
Additions to national income	
Government transfers to persons	41,075
Net interest paid by government and by consumers	22,248
Accrued gains on farm assets and nonfarm real estate	35,280
Corporation inventory valuation adjustment	1,356
Total additions	99,959
Deductions from national income	
Transfers to persons outside the family household population	7,016
Interest payments to persons and institutions outside the family household population	4,495
Corporation profits tax and inventory gains of fiduciaries, pension funds, and non-profit organizations	18,429
Earnings of persons in the military and institutional population and selected imputed items	12,725
Proprietors' and rental income received by fiduciaries, pension funds, and nonprofit organizations	2,889
Imputed interest from services of banks and financial intermediaries and other adjustments	15,224
Total deductions	60,778
Family income	**659,766**

Sources: *Survey of Current Business*, Vol. 50 (July 1970), Table 1.9; U.S. Department of Commerce, Bureau of Economic Analysis, unpublished worksheets; and authors' estimates.

for 1966, were appended to the MERGE file without any of the SEO demographic data.

Adjusting the Income Components

Since the total income recorded in the SEO and tax files was less than the estimated aggregate family income, the final step in creating the MERGE file was to adjust the income components to add up to the national aggregates. The major adjustments are shown in the aggregate in Table A-1 and by income source in Tables A-2 and A-3.[8]

The adjustments to the national totals were allocated to individual family units in the file on the basis of a wide variety of data. For most income sources, there were independent estimates of the number of recipients of such income. If the number of recipients was close to the

[8] A working paper with complete details on the methods used to derive the income aggregates and to distribute the adjustments to the national income totals is available on request.

TABLE A-2. Relation between National Income and Family Income, by Source, 1966

Millions of dollars

Source of income	National income	Net adjustments	Family income
Compensation of employees	**435,504**	**−12,725**	**422,779**
Wages and salaries	394,499	−12,897	381,602
Supplements to wages and salaries	41,005	172	41,177
Employer contributions for social insurance	(20,294)	(−388)	(19,906)
Other labor income	(20,711)	(560)	(21,271)
Proprietors' income	**61,299**	**−2,897**	**58,402**
Business and professional	45,214	−648	44,566
Farm	16,085	−2,249	13,836
Rental income	**19,955**	**8**	**19,963**
Corporate profits and inventory valuation adjustment	**82,440**	**−18,429**	**64,011**
Profits tax liability	34,281	−8,227	26,054
Dividends	20,797	−4,991	15,806
Undistributed profits	29,146	−6,995	22,151
Inventory valuation adjustment	−1,784	1,784	...
Net interest	**21,387**	**2,529**	**23,916**
Government transfers to persons	...	**34,059**	**34,059**
Accrued gains on farm assets and nonfarm real estate	...	**35,280**	**35,280**
Corporation inventory evaluation adjustment	...	**1,356**	**1,356**
Total	**620,585**	**39,181**	**659,766**

Sources: *Survey of Current Business*, Vol. 50 (July 1970), Table 1.10; U.S. Department of Commerce, Bureau of Economic Analysis, unpublished worksheets; and authors' estimates.

number in the original SEO file and the aggregate amount of income was too low, the difference between the national aggregate and the MERGE file total was attributed solely to underreporting. In such cases, the original MERGE file amount was adjusted proportionately to yield the national aggregate. If the number of recipients and the aggregate income were both too low, the difference was attributed to nonreporting and underreporting. In these cases, family units that originally reported no income from the source were allocated such income. The selection of these families was based on relevant information in the file for the sample units and the eligibility criteria for receiving such income. To the family units so selected average amounts of income were imputed on the basis of aggregate statistics. Amounts initially reported by sample units were assumed to be underreported; and these were blown up to equal the national income aggregate less the amount imputed to nonreporters.

In addition to the imputations made to correct for errors due to nonresponse, it was necessary to add information to the MERGE file that was not available from the SEO or from tax returns. The items that were imputed and the basis of imputation were as follows. Net imputed rent was allocated on the basis of the equity in owner-occupied homes reported

TABLE A-3. Relation between Personal Income and Family Income, by Source, 1966

Millions of dollars

Source of income	Personal income	Adjustments	Family income
Employee compensation	**397,469**	**25,310**	**422,779**
Wage and salary disbursements	394,499	−12,897	381,602
Personal contributions for social insurance	−17,741	37,647	19,906
Other labor income	20,711	560	21,271
Proprietors' income	**61,299**	**−2,897**	**58,402**
Business and professional	45,214	−648	44,566
Farm	16,085	−2,249	13,836
Rental income	**19,955**	**8**	**19,963**
Corporate earnings	**20,797**[a]	**43,214**[b]	**64,011**[b]
Interest	**43,635**	**−19,719**	**23,916**
Transfer payments	**44,061**	**−10,002**	**34,059**
Accrued capital gains on business inventories, farm assets, and nonfarm real estate	...	**36,636**	**36,636**
Total	587,216	72,550	659,766

Sources: *Survey of Current Business*, Vol. 50 (July 1970), Tables 1.9, 1.10, and 2.1; and U.S. Department of Commerce, Bureau of Economic Analysis, unpublished worksheets.
[a] Includes corporate dividends only.
[b] Includes corporation income tax and undistributed profits.

by respondents. Wage supplements were distributed on the basis of the occupational, industrial, and wage characteristics reported by the survey units. State-local tax-exempt bond interest was allocated on the basis of the distribution of state-local bond ownership shown in the Federal Reserve Board's 1963 Survey of Financial Characteristics.[9] Accrued asset gains were distributed on the basis of realized capital gains and property income reported on tax returns.

Finally, in order to compare the distributions of tax burdens, it was necessary to derive the income amounts that apply for each set of incidence assumptions. The steps in the derivation are shown in Table A-4. For variants under which it is assumed that part of the corporation income tax and payroll tax is shifted to consumption, the shifted part was deducted from family income because it becomes the equivalent of an indirect business tax. For those variants that assume that part (or all) of the property tax is borne by property income, that portion of the tax was included in family income and was deducted from indirect business taxes. The final adjustment was to add indirect business taxes to family income in order to arrive at adjusted family income. This adjustment was made by multiplying the family income of each unit in the MERGE file by the ratio of estimated total adjusted family income to total family income.

[9] Dorothy S. Projector and Gertrude S. Weiss, *Survey of Financial Characteristics of Consumers* (Board of Governors of the Federal Reserve System, 1966).

TABLE A-4. Derivation of Adjusted Family Income under Various Incidence Assumptions, 1966

Millions of dollars

Item	Variant							
	1a	1b	1c	2a	2b	3a	3b	3c
Family income as derived from national income accounts	659,766	659,766	659,766	659,766	659,766	659,766	659,766	659,766
Minus: Corporation income tax in national income accounts	−26,067	−26,067	−26,067	−26,067	−26,067	−26,067	−26,067	−26,067
Subtotal	633,699	633,699	633,699	633,699	633,699	633,699	633,699	633,699
Corporation income tax allocated to:								
Corporate stockholders	30,167	...	13,034	26,067	26,067	13,034	...	13,034
Property income in general	...	30,167	15,084	...	...	...	15,084	15,084
Corporate compensation	...	...	...	...	...	8,570	...	...
Payroll tax (portion of payroll tax assumed to be shifted to consumption)	...	...	...	...	−8,092	...	−8,092	...
Property taxes allocated to:								
Property income in general	15,036	21,651	21,651	...	...	...	...	7,518
Landowners (tax on site value)	7,517	...	...	7,517	7,517	7,517	7,517	7,517
Family income for each set of incidence assumptions	686,419	685,517	683,468	667,283	659,191	662,820	648,208	676,852
Indirect business taxes								
Property taxes	...	...	...	17,086	17,086	17,086	17,086	8,543
Federal excise taxes	12,691	12,691	12,691	12,691	12,691	12,691	12,691	12,691
State-local sales and excise taxes	23,956	23,956	23,956	23,956	23,956	23,956	23,956	23,956
Taxes treated as indirect taxes								
Corporation income tax	...	...	...	...	...	8,570	17,140	...
Payroll tax	...	...	...	...	8,092	...	8,092	...
Adjusted family income	723,066	722,164	720,115	721,016	721,016	725,123	727,173	722,042

Sources: Tables A-1, B-1, B-2; and U.S. Department of Commerce, Bureau of Economic Analysis, unpublished worksheets. Slight differences may occur in numbers appearing in other tables in this study because of rounding.

Taxes and Their Allocation

THE DERIVATION OF total taxes as defined in this study and the distribution of these amounts by income classes involved a large number of calculations and assumptions. This appendix explains the detailed procedures used (1) in estimating total taxes from the official statistics on government receipts, (2) in adjusting the totals to the definitions implied by the various incidence assumptions, and (3) in distributing each tax among the nation's family units.

Government Receipts and Taxes

Government receipts, as reported in the national income accounts, include a large number of items that are not really taxes. The first adjustment made to the published statistics was to remove all the fees and charges that are included in federal and state-local personal and business nontax receipts and the few items (such as dog and marriage license fees) that are included in state-local personal tax receipts.

Estate, gift, and death tax receipts are not included in tax receipts because there is no reliable statistical basis for allocating them among family units.[1]

Federal customs duties are not included in taxes as defined here because they are not levied primarily for purposes of revenue raising. The total amount of customs duties collected in 1966 was small, and

---

[1] However, the results of a rough attempt to make such a distribution are reported in Appendix C.

TABLE B-1. Derivation of Federal Taxes from Total National Income Receipts, by Source, 1966

Millions of dollars

Source	National income receipts	Adjustments	Tax receipts[a]
Personal tax and nontax receipts	61,705	−3,128	58,577
Income taxes	58,577	. . .	58,577
Estate and gift taxes	3,080	−3,080	. . .
Nontaxes	48	−48	. . .
Corporate profits tax accruals	32,072	−7,685	24,387
Indirect business tax and nontax accruals	15,714	−3,023	12,691
Gasoline excise taxes	2,905	. . .	2,905
Liquor excise taxes	4,026	. . .	4,026
Tobacco excise taxes	2,110	. . .	2,110
Other excise taxes (minus refunds)	3,650	. . .	3,650
Customs duties	1,930	−1,930	. . .
Nontaxes	1,093	−1,093	. . .
Payroll taxes	33,044	−3,048	29,996
Total	142,535	−16,884	125,651

Sources: U.S. Department of Commerce, *Survey of Current Business*, Vol. 50 (July 1970), Tables 3.1, 3.8; and U.S. Department of Commerce, Office of Business Economics, unpublished worksheets.
a As defined in this study.

their inclusion or exclusion would not materially affect the results of the study.

The adjustments of corporation income tax receipts reflect estimates of the amounts allocated to nonprofit institutions, fiduciaries, and other stockholders that are not included in the family household population.[2]

The final adjustment was to subtract from government receipts contributions from governments and from employees to pension and insurance plans since these are more in the nature of insurance payments than of taxes. These contributions include payments to the federal civilian employee retirement systems and to the national veterans' life insurance trust funds. For the same reason contributions to state and local government retirement systems were also subtracted.

The effects of all the adjustments are shown in Tables B-1 and B-2. Tax revenues of all units of government amounted to $183.5 billion in 1966, $30 billion less than total government receipts as defined in the national income accounts. Federal taxes were about $17 billion less than total receipts, and state-local taxes were $13 billion less. These particular amounts apply only to the national income incidence assumptions (Variant 2a).

[2] For the derivation of this adjustment, see pages 96 and 98.

TABLE B-2. Derivation of State and Local Taxes from Total National Income Receipts, by Source, 1966

Millions of dollars

Source	National income receipts	Adjustments	Tax receipts[a]
Personal tax and nontax receipts	13,659	−6,286	7,373
Income taxes	5,422	...	5,422
Death and gift taxes	832	−832	...
Motor vehicle licenses	1,131	...	1,131
Property taxes	820	...	820
Miscellaneous[b]	266	−266	...
Nontaxes	5,188	−5,188	...
Corporate profits tax accruals	2,209	−529	1,680
Indirect business tax and nontax accruals	49,938	−1,379	48,559
General sales taxes	10,603	...	10,603
Gasoline excise taxes	4,778	...	4,778
Liquor excise taxes	1,012	...	1,012
Tobacco excise taxes	1,584	...	1,584
Motor vehicle licenses	1,086	...	1,086
Property taxes	24,603	...	24,603
Other taxes	4,893	...	4,893
Nontaxes	1,379	−1,379	...
Payroll taxes	4,991	−4,705	286
Total[c]	70,797	−12,899	57,898

Sources: *Survey of Current Business*, Vol. 50 (July 1970), Tables 3.3, 3.8; and authors' estimate.
a As defined in this study.
b Includes marriage license fees, charges for dog licenses, and the like.
c Excludes federal grants-in-aid.

Taxes under Various Incidence Assumptions

The total tax amounts paid by families in the household sector vary somewhat under the different incidence assumptions examined in this study. Since personal income, sales and excise, and employee payroll taxes are the same under the various incidence assumptions, the differences among the tax aggregates result from the assumptions used to allocate the property tax, the corporation income tax, and the employer payroll tax.[3] The methods used to derive the aggregates for each set of assumptions are explained in this section.

Corporation Income Tax

The corporation income tax was assumed to be borne: (1) entirely by stockholders under Variants 2a and 2b; (2) by property owners in

[3] See Chapter 2, pages 39–41.

general under Variants 1a and 1b; (3) partly by stockholders and partly by property owners in general under Variants 1c and 3c; and (4) partly by one of the former groups, with some shifting to workers or consumers under Variants 3a and 3b. Not only do these variants involve allocations of the corporation income tax among different families, they also require the allocation of different amounts of tax.

In 1966 federal and state corporation tax accruals were $34.3 billion.[4] When part of the tax was assumed to be shifted to workers or consumers, the amount shifted was calculated as a percentage of the $34.3 billion total. Thus, under Variants 3a and 3b, either one-half or one-fourth of the total ($17.1 billion or $8.6 billion) was distributed to consumption, and under 3a one-fourth was shifted to compensation. When the tax was allocated to stockholders or property-income recipients in general, the total amount distributed to families changed because part of corporate earnings and of property income is not received by families in the household sector. When the tax was allocated among stockholders, only 76 percent of the total ($26.1 billion) was the amount used. When the tax was assumed to be borne by recipients of property income in general, 88 percent ($30.2 billion) was allocated. The amounts for each of the incidence variants are shown in Table B-3.

The amount of corporation tax allocated to families, on the assumption that the tax is borne by stockholders, was based on the proportion of total dividends received by each household unit. Nonprofit institutions, pension funds, fiduciaries, and others not represented in the household sector received an estimated 24 percent of total dividends paid in 1966. It was assumed, therefore, that families owned 76 percent of total corporate stock in the United States.[5]

Ownership of property in general was based on income from property of families in the household sector. The items included in property income are interest, rent (including imputed rent), royalties, corporate earnings allocated to households (including dividends and retained earnings, but *not* the corporation income tax), accrued farm asset gains, and accrued nonfarm real estate gains.[6] In addition, part of the net income from farm

---

[4] U.S. Department of Commerce, *Survey of Current Business,* Vol. 50 (July 1970), Table 1.10.

[5] The data were obtained from unpublished worksheets of the Office of Business Economics, U.S. Department of Commerce. Since there was no direct information on assets owned, it is assumed throughout the study that income from property is a reliable indicator of property value. It is recognized that this does not take account of nonearning assets, but the omission does not seriously distort the results.

[6] Ideally, the allocation should have been based on income shares as they would have been before any taxes were imposed. Since these amounts cannot be observed, it was assumed that the relative shares could be approximated by the net receipts *after* the corporation income tax, but *before* the personal income tax.

TABLE B-3. Federal, State, and Local Taxes under Various Incidence Assumptions, by Source, 1966

Millions of dollars

Source and allocation	Incidence variant							
	1a	1b	1c	2a	2b	3a	3b	3c
Individual income tax	63,999	63,999	63,999	63,999	63,999	63,999	63,999	63,999
Corporation income tax								
To dividends	...	30,167	...	26,067	26,067	...	...	...
To property income in general	30,167	...	...	...	...	...	...	...
Half to dividends, half to property income	...	...	28,118	...	...	...	...	28,118
Half to dividends, one-quarter to consumption, one-quarter to corporate compensation	...	...	...	...	...	30,174	32,224	...
Half to property income, half to consumption								
Personal property tax and motor vehicle licenses	1,951	1,951	1,951	1,951	1,951	1,951	1,951	1,951
Property tax on land								
To landowners	7,518	...	...	7,518	7,518	7,518	7,518	7,518
To property income in general	...	6,616	6,616	...	...	...	...	...
Property tax on improvements								
To shelter and consumption	15,035	...	...	17,085	17,085	17,085	17,085	...
To property income in general	...	15,035	15,035	...	...	...	...	...
Half to shelter and consumption, half to property income in general	...	...	...	...	...	...	...	16,060
Sales and excise taxes	36,647	36,647	36,647	36,647	36,647	36,647	36,647	36,647
Payroll tax on employees	14,088	14,088	14,088	14,088	14,088	14,088	14,088	14,088
Payroll tax on employers								
To employee compensation	16,194	16,194	16,194	16,194	16,194	16,194	...	16,194
Half to employee compensation, half to consumption	...	...	...	...	...	...	16,194	...
Total	185,599	184,697	182,648	183,549	183,549	187,656	189,706	184,575

Sources: Authors' estimates based on U.S. Department of Commerce, Office of Business Economics, unpublished worksheets. For an explanation of the incidence variants, see Table 3-1. Slight differences may occur in numbers appearing in other tables in this study because of rounding.

and nonfarm self employment was considered to be a return on capital used in the business.[7] In total, 88 percent of all property income accrues to families in the household sector, and this was used to estimate the amount of corporation income tax to be distributed to families under the appropriate incidence variants.

After the amount of corporation income tax to be distributed for each incidence variant was computed, the tax was allocated among family units in the MERGE file in proportion either to dividend income or to property income received by each unit. When it was assumed that part of the tax was shifted to workers, that part was distributed in proportion to the total compensation of corporation employees.[8] When part of the corporation income tax was assumed to be borne by consumers, the distribution among families was based on their estimated total money consumption.[9]

As was shown in Table B-3, the amount of the corporation income tax distributed to families in 1966 under the eight incidence assumptions differs considerably, ranging from $26.1 billion under Variants 2a and 2b to $32.2 billion under Variant 3b. In addition to the effect of differences in the aggregate, the incidence of the corporation income tax by income classes reflects the effects of the different incidence assumptions. Thus the incidence of the corporation income tax is substantially less progressive under Variant 3b than under the other variants because half of the tax is assumed to be borne by consumers and the total amount of tax distributed to families is highest.

[7] The proportions used were 29 percent of net farm profit and 14 percent of net profit on nonfarm business. The proportions are based on unpublished estimates by Edward F. Denison. The amounts of total money property income received by nonprofit institutions and others not represented in the family population were derived from unpublished worksheets of the U.S. Department of Commerce, Office of Business Economics. The proportions for the small amounts of nonmoney return on property were estimated by the authors.

[8] It was possible to make a rough division of compensation between corporate and noncorporate employment on the basis of information on the industry and occupation of workers available in the original Survey of Economic Opportunity (SEO). Farm workers, service workers in industries that are not heavily corporate, and similar groups of employees were assumed to be noncorporate; all other workers were assumed to be employed in the corporate sector.

[9] It was not considered feasible to try to estimate for individual families what proportion of their total consumption involved commodities produced by corporations. Consequently no distinction was made between consumption goods originating in (or processed at some stage of their production by) corporations and those that were entirely noncorporate. See page 101 for a more detailed explanation of the consumption estimates.

Property Tax

Like the corporation income tax, the amount of the property tax paid by families in the household sector varies with the assumption used. The entire tax is borne by families if it is assumed that the property tax is a tax on shelter and consumption; but part of the tax is borne by nonprofit institutions and other groups if the tax is in whole or in part a tax on property income. Moreover, because the incidence of the taxes on the site value of land and on structures and improvements was assumed to be different under six of the eight variants, it was necessary to estimate these two components of property tax collections and to allocate them separately among family units.

State-local property tax collections reported in the national income accounts amounted to $25.4 billion in 1966. This is the sum of $820 million of personal property taxes, which are regarded as personal tax receipts in the national income accounts, and $24.6 billion of real property taxes, which are regarded as indirect business tax accruals.[10]

The $820 million of personal property taxes consists primarily of taxes on automobiles and household furnishings belonging to individuals. Because there was no information on the value of family household furnishings subject to tax in the MERGE file, personal property taxes were distributed among families on the basis of the value of automobiles reported in the SEO. The distribution is the same under all the incidence variants.

The first step in allocating real property taxes to families in the file was to divide the $24.6 billion total among amounts collected on property owned by nonfarm households, on farms, and on nonfarm business enterprises. These estimates were based on 1966 property values in a study by Allen D. Manvel.[11] The estimated collections by sector were $9.5 billion from nonfarm housing; $4.1 billion from farmers; and $10.9 billion from nonfarm business. For each sector, the total was allocated between taxes collected on land and those collected on structures, on the basis of the Manvel data.[12] (See Table B-4.)

---

[10] For national income accounting purposes, homeowners are considered to be in the business of renting their own dwelling units.

[11] "Trends in the Value of Real Estate and Land, 1956 to 1966," in *Three Land Research Studies,* Prepared for the Consideration of the National Commission on Urban Problems (U.S. Government Printing Office, 1968), pp. 1–17. Taxes were allocated on the basis of market value rather than of assessed valuations. It was felt that, on the average, the effective tax rate on market value is more reliable than the rate on assessed valuation, which varies widely both within and among jurisdictions.

[12] *Ibid.,* p. 6.

TABLE B-4. Estimated State and Local Real Property Tax Collections, by Sector, 1966

Dollar amounts in millions

Sector	Tax on land	Tax on improvements	Total tax	Tax on land as percentage of total
Nonfarm, single family housing	$2,568	$6,944	$9,512	27.0
Farms	2,967	1,175	4,142	71.6
Nonfarm business	1,983	8,966	10,949	18.1
Multiple family housing	350	1,400	1,750	20.0
All other nonfarm business	1,633	7,566	9,199	17.8
All sectors	7,518	17,085	24,603	30.6

Sources: Authors' estimates based on U.S. Department of Commerce, Office of Business Economics, unpublished worksheets; and Allen D. Manvel, "Trends in the Value of Real Estate and Land, 1956 to 1966," *Three Land Research Studies*, Prepared for the Consideration of the National Commission on Urban Problems (U.S. Government Printing Office, 1968), pp. 1–17.

In allocating the $7.5 billion of property tax collected on land two different assumptions were used: (1) that the tax is borne by landowners; and (2) that it is borne by owners of property in general. On the first assumption, the tax on the site value of land was distributed among home-owners, farmers, and owners of business property in proportion to the gross value of property as reported in the SEO. On the second assumption, 88 percent of the $7.5 billion was distributed among all families on the basis of property income (the same basis that was used to distribute the corporation income tax on this assumption).[13]

The $17.1 billion of property tax collected on structures and improvements was distributed on the following assumptions: (1) that it is borne by shelter and consumption; (2) that it is borne by property income in general; and (3) that half is borne by shelter and consumption and half by property income in general. On the first assumption the $6.9 billion of taxes on nonfarm dwellings was distributed to homeowners on the basis of the gross value of their housing (since they would bear this in their role as tenants renting from themselves), and the $1.4 billion of property taxes on multiple family housing was allocated to renters in proportion to the rental payments they reported in the SEO. The $8.7 billion of taxes on structures and improvements used in agriculture and nonfarm businesses was allocated among all families in proportion to their total money consumption (excluding rent).

On the assumption that taxes on structures are borne by owners of capital in general, $15.0 billion (88 percent of $17.1 billion) was allocated among all units in proportion to their property income. The third

[13] See pages 96 and 98.

incidence assumption is simply a combination of the first two: $8.5 billion (50 percent of $17.1 billion) was allocated to shelter and consumption, and $7.5 billion (50 percent of $15.0 billion) was distributed among property income recipients.

Payroll Taxes

Employer payroll taxes for social security, unemployment insurance, and workmen's compensation were assumed to be borne by employees under all the incidence variants except Variants 2b and 3b. In these cases, half the employer tax payments under these programs was assumed to be shifted forward to consumers. Therefore, one-half of total employer payroll tax payments was allocated to families on the basis of their total money consumption.

The social security payroll tax on employees was assumed to be borne by workers under all the variants. These taxes were calculated on the basis of the earnings of employees and the self-employed in the MERGE file.

Sales and Excise Taxes

General and selective sales taxes were assumed to be borne by consumers under all of the incidence variants used in the study. Since consumption data were not collected in the SEO, estimates of consumption for each family unit were added to the file in order to allocate these taxes.

The consumption estimates were based on consumption data collected in the U.S. Bureau of Labor Statistics' 1960–61 Survey of Consumer Expenditures. The 1960–61 data were projected to 1966 income and consumption levels for eleven major demographic groups of families on the assumption that the ratios of consumption to income would be the same at the same *relative* levels in the income distribution. After aggregate consumption was projected to the 1966 level, separate projections within the total were made for each of several consumption items (such as alcohol, tobacco, gasoline) that are subject to special excise taxes. This was also done by assuming the same consumption patterns for families at the same relative income levels in 1960–61 and 1966. An examination of the distributional results, and comparison of the totals with national income aggregates for 1966, indicated that this method gave reasonable results.

Taxes in the MERGE File

The tax amounts presented in Table B-3 above are based on control figures derived from the official national income accounts. The actual tax amounts recorded in the MERGE file differ slightly from the control

TABLE B-5. Comparison of Control and MERGE File Tax Amounts, by Source, National Income Incidence Assumptions, 1966

Millions of dollars

Source	Control amount	MERGE amount	Difference
Individual income tax	63,999	60,806	3,193
Corporation income tax	26,067	26,068	−1
Property taxes	26,554	26,556	−2
Tax on personal property and motor vehicle licenses	1,951	1,952	−1
Land tax	7,518	7,520	−2
Tax on improvements	17,085	17,084	1
Sales and excise taxes	36,647	36,647	. . .
Payroll taxes, employee	14,088	13,299	789
Payroll taxes, employer	16,194	18,477	−2,283
Total	183,549	181,853	1,696

Sources: Table B-3 (Variant 2a), and the MERGE data file.

amounts. As is shown in Table B-5, the difference between the control and the MERGE tax totals is only about $1.7 billion, or 0.9 percent, but this is the net effect of two larger offsetting differences.[14]

The first significant discrepancy is the $3.2 billion difference between the control and MERGE amounts for the individual income tax. The $64.0 billion control amount is comprised of $58.6 billion of federal taxes and $5.4 billion of state and local government taxes. The MERGE file contains the amount of federal tax reported by each taxpaying unit in 1966, but these amounts add to $55.4 billion rather than the $58.6 billion figure in the national income accounts. Since the reported amount was equal to about 95 percent of the control figure, the MERGE file figures were accepted, and no effort was made to adjust them to the higher control total.[15] It was felt that any arbitrary attempt to distribute the $3.2 billion difference among family units might distort the relationship between income tax payments and personal income.

State-local income tax payments in the MERGE file are equal to the $5.4 billion control total. Approximately 75 percent of the total was reported by those who itemized their deductions on federal income tax returns. For units that did not itemize, state-local income tax payments

[14] The slight differences for the corporation income and property taxes represent only rounding errors that result from the distribution of identical totals to the family units in the MERGE file. Such differences are inevitable and are not significant.

[15] An unknown, but probably small, part of the difference can be attributed to the fact that the SEO population differs from the national income coverage.

TABLE B-6. Comparison of Control and MERGE File Taxes, Adjusted Family Income, and Effective Tax Rates under Various Incidence Variants, 1966

Dollar amounts in millions; tax rates in percent

Incidence variant	Total taxes		Adjusted family income		Effective tax rates	
	Control	MERGE	Control	MERGE	Control	MERGE
1a	$185,599	$183,898	$723,066	$721,378	25.67	25.49
1b	184,697	182,992	722,164	720,472	25.58	25.40
1c	182,648	180,945	720,115	718,425	25.36	25.19
2a	183,549	181,853	721,016	719,334	25.46	25.28
2b	183,549	181,852	721,016	719,332	25.46	25.28
3a	187,656	185,959	725,123	723,439	25.88	25.70
3b	189,706	188,007	727,173	725,485	26.09	25.91
3c	184,575	182,838	722,042	720,356	25.56	25.38

Sources: Authors' estimates based on U.S. Department of Commerce, Office of Business Economics, unpublished worksheets; the MERGE data file; and Appendix Tables A-4 and B-3. For an explanation of the incidence variants, see Table 3-1.

were estimated and distributed among units on the basis of income, family size, and place of residence.[16]

The other large discrepancy shown in Table B-5 is a $1.5 billion difference between the national income control and MERGE file payroll tax amounts. Since neither employee nor employer payroll tax data were available in the SEO or tax files that were used to construct the MERGE file, these taxes were estimated on the basis of workers' earnings, industry and occupation, and the 1966 tax rates. Social security tax payments by self-employed individuals were taken directly from the tax file.

As can be seen in Table B-5, the amount calculated for employee payments was $800 million less than the national income total, while the calculated employer contributions were almost $2.3 billion larger than the control amount. Again it was felt that any arbitrary method of allocating these amounts among family units might distort the relationship between these taxes and earnings, and the MERGE file amounts were not adjusted to the control totals.

For the other taxes, the control totals were distributed according to the various criteria described earlier. Therefore, aside from rounding, there is no discrepancy between the MERGE file and the national income totals for these taxes.

The effective rates of tax, based on income and tax data in the MERGE file, and the control totals derived from the national income accounts are shown in Table B-6. As may be seen by comparing the figures in the last two columns of the table, there are only slight differences in the overall effective rates of tax for any of the incidence variants. There is little reason to believe that the major findings of this study are affected appreciably by these differences.

---

[16] The last criterion was needed because not all states had an individual income tax. In 1966 seventeen states did not levy a personal income tax.

APPENDIX C

Distribution of Burdens Including Death and Gift Taxes

EVEN THOUGH AN economic definition of income would include them, receipts from gifts and bequests are excluded from the concept of adjusted family income used in this study. (See Chapter 2.) They were omitted because the data available are not reliable for estimating the aggregate amounts or their distribution among families. Nevertheless, an attempt was made to prepare such estimates on a rough basis in order to determine what effect including receipts from gifts and bequests in income might have on the distribution of tax burdens by income classes. The procedures used and the results for the two extreme incidence variants (1c and 3b) used in the study are described in this appendix.

In 1966 the total amount of wealth distributed in the form of bequests was about $64.7 billion.[1] Since the necessary information for distributing this large amount according to the income classes of the recipients was not available, it was allocated on the basis of the adjusted gross income of families in the MERGE file, with an arbitrary modification to prevent what was regarded as an excessively large concentration of bequests in the low-income classes.[2]

---

[1] Gifts, which are small relative to bequests, were ignored. The estimate for bequests was based on the Internal Revenue Service estate tax data file. The assistance of James D. Smith of Pennsylvania State University in the preparation of this estimate is gratefully acknowledged.

[2] Unpublished data from the Survey Research Center of the University of Michigan indicate that the size of taxable estate increases with income for high-income recipients. Cumulative quintiles of income were calculated for families with

TABLE C-1. Effect of Federal and State Estate and Gift Taxes on Effective Rates of Tax under Incidence Variants 1c and 3b, by Adjusted Family Income Class, 1966

Income classes in thousands of dollars; tax rates in percent

	Variant 1c		Variant 3b	
Adjusted family income	Excluding estate and gift taxes	Including estate and gift taxes[a]	Excluding estate and gift taxes	Including estate and gift taxes[a]
0–3	18.7	18.7	28.1	28.1
3–5	20.4	20.3	25.2	25.2
5–10	22.6	22.6	25.9	25.9
10–15	22.8	22.8	25.5	25.5
15–20	23.2	23.1	25.3	25.2
20–25	23.9	23.4	25.1	24.6
25–30	25.1	23.4	24.3	22.8
30–50	26.0	21.2	24.3	19.8
50–100	29.8	19.2	26.2	16.7
100–500	40.0	32.5	29.8	24.6
500–1,000	46.7	42.2	29.8	30.5
1,000 and over	50.8	47.3	32.4	35.2
All classes[b]	25.2	23.6	25.9	24.3

Source: Computed from the 1966 MERGE data file. For an explanation of the incidence variants, see Table 3-1.
[a] Effective tax rates are based on adjusted family income plus bequests.
[b] Includes negative incomes not shown separately.

After the total was allocated, federal and state death and gift taxes were calculated for families receiving bequests of more than the $60,000 that is exempted from the federal estate tax. The federal taxes were obtained by applying the effective estate tax rates on federal estate tax returns to the taxable bequests.[3] State death tax amounts were allocated proportionally to the estimated amount of federal estate tax.[4] Gift taxes were also distributed in this manner. The 1966 estate and gift taxes amounted to $3.9 billion, or about 6 percent of the estimated bequests.

The effect on the progressivity of Variants 1c and 3b of including

---

income above $30,000, and taxable estates were distributed on this basis. Thus a second quintile family received a second quintile estate amount. The nontaxable estates were allocated in a log-normal fashion to families with incomes under $30,000.

[3] These effective rates were obtained from U.S. Internal Revenue Service, *Statistics of Income—1965, Fiduciary, Gift, and Estate Tax Returns* (1967).

[4] This assumes that state death taxes have the same structure as the federal tax. While this is obviously not the case, it was the only practical procedure available for allocating the state taxes.

wealth transfers and transfer taxes in income and taxes is small.[5] (See Table C-1.) Under 1c, the gifts and bequests that were added to adjusted family income were proportionately larger than the increase in taxes, thus leaving unchanged or *reducing* overall effective rates at all levels of income. However, the reduction in the effective rates is largest (in percentage points) in the top income classes, so that the progressivity of Variant 1c is reduced. In the case of 3b, the effective rates for those at the lowest end of the income scale were unchanged, those in the middle to high range were reduced, and those at the very top were increased. On balance, progressivity is increased somewhat under 3b.

[5] Since gifts were omitted from income while the gift taxes were included in taxes, the effective tax rates shown are slightly overstated.

Multivariate Statistical Analysis of Factors Affecting Relative Tax Rates

IN CHAPTER 5 effective tax rates were computed separately on the basis of various economic and demographic characteristics. This appendix summarizes the results of a statistical analysis that was undertaken to distinguish more clearly the factors that tend to produce low and high effective tax rates.

Methodology

The analysis was made using the Automatic Interaction Detector (AID) computer program.[1] As is indicated by its name, the program is particularly useful for analyzing data where an interaction effect exists, that is, where the explanatory or "causal" variables do not act independently and additively in explaining the dependent variable. This may occur for a number of reasons: (1) the effect of one factor may depend on the level of another; (2) any particular causal variable may affect only one part of the population; or (3) several explanations may apply, as when any one of two or three circumstances produces a given result.

---

[1] For a full explanation of the program with examples, see John A. Sonquist, Elizabeth Lauh Baker, and James N. Morgan, *Searching for Structure* (University of Michigan, Survey Research Center, 1971). The description of the program in this section draws heavily on that presented by Robin Barlow, Harvey E. Brazer, and James N. Morgan in *Economic Behavior of the Affluent* (Brookings Institution, 1966), pp. 266–69.

The AID computer program imposes no restrictions on the data except that the dependent variable—the observation to be explained—must be a reasonably normally distributed variable; if it is a ratio, the proportions should not be too close to zero or to 100 percent.

The program operates sequentially. It first examines the effect on the whole sample of each explanatory characteristic in turn, finding the best way of using that factor to divide the sample into two groups. "Best" means the division that reduces the unexplained sum of squared deviations (or "error variance") the most. Using two subgroup averages instead of one overall average to predict the dependent variable reduces the predictive error, and the process identifies the largest such reduction. The test is a test of importance, not significance. Not only must the two groups so formed be different, they must also each contain a substantial number of cases. Within each of the two groups, the individuals are more like one another (homogeneous) than they are like those in the other group. Where the explanatory characteristic has a natural ordering (such as income), that order can be preserved; but it is also possible to allow the program to discern the best re-ranking and the best division of the sample on the basis of a new ordering.

After the first division, the program recalls which predictor's best split is better than that of any of the other predictors and divides the entire population into two subgroups on that basis. Each of the two subgroups thus generated is examined in the same way, using all the predictors, and is split again. Each of those new groups is then examined in turn and split if possible. The new groups spread out like the branches of a tree, each containing fewer cases and each split doing its best to maximize the explained variance (that is, minimize the unexplained variance).

The process stops when no division of a group can reduce the unexplained sum of squares (variance) by as much as some predetermined criterion level, usually 5 percent, or when a subgroup would contain less than 1 percent of the original total sum of squares around the mean. It also stops when any of the subgroups produced would be so small that there would be a serious question as to the sampling reliability of the results. Some of the branches end before others, of course, and different predictors are used in different branches.

If a particular predictor has no apparent effect either over the whole population or on any of the major subgroups generated, one can be reasonably sure it does not matter. (The program prints out the subgroup averages according to each predictor at each stage.) But even this certainty is reduced where there are two predictors that are correlated with one another. With the sequential approach, once the sample is divided on the basis of the more important predictor, the other is often unable to assume any importance at all.[2]

The results of the AID process are independent of the order in which the variables are introduced, but they do depend on which variables are introduced into the analysis and on the precision with which they are measured. It is always possible that a different variable, or a better measure of the characteristic than the one already used, would produce different results.

Results of the AID Analysis

The AID analysis was run separately for incidence Variants 1c and 3b. In both cases, the dependent variable was the effective rate of tax. The independent variables that could have been used in explaining differences in rates included all the economic and demographic characteristics discussed in Chapter 5[3] plus the absolute amount of adjusted family income (AFI).[4]

Although all six sets of independent variables could have been chosen as predictors, in fact only three or four were used in the analysis for each incidence variant. Three of the sets of explanatory variables are common to both analyses: marital status-family size, major income source, and income amount. In addition, the urban-rural variable was used in 3b.

Variant 1c results. The AID analysis results under Variant 1c are presented in Table D-1. As shown, the distinction between transfer payments and all other major income sources was the most important variable for explaining differences in effective tax rates under Variant 1c assumptions. Following this in order of importance was amount of income (under and over $1,500) and marital status. Except for families with very low incomes, having property as the major source of income was also a significant factor in explaining effective tax rates. In fact, for those with AFI of $1,500 or more, the highest average rates were paid by those whose

[2] On the other hand, with multiple regression both predictors would show some apparent effect, dividing up the credit, but the sampling errors would tend to become large.

[3] These were age of family head (under or over age 65), housing status (homeowner-renter), source of income among four major groupings (ninety-four families with no major income source were excluded from the analyses), marital status and family size, and urban-rural place of residence.

[4] Fourteen income classes were used in the analyses. Groupings of $1,500 to $2,500 were used up to the $10,000 level, $5,000 classes were used between the $10,000 and $40,000 income levels, and broader classes were used for incomes of $40,000 and over.

TABLE D-1. Factors Associated with Differences in Effective Tax Rates, Incidence Variant 1c, 1966

Explanatory variable	Average effective tax rate (percent)[a]	Number of cases as a weighted percentage of entire sample	Unweighted number of cases[b]
Entire sample	22.8	100.0	71,940
Major income source: transfers	13.4	12.4	4,108
Major income source: wages, business, or property	24.1	87.6	67,832
Adjusted family income: under $1,500	52.1	2.3	918
Major income source: wages	31.1	1.5	634
Major income source: business or property	95.3	0.7	284
Adjusted family income: $1,500 or more	23.3	85.3	66,914
Major income source: wages or business	22.7	75.9	40,635
Single or married with less than two children	24.0	43.1	20,839
Single	27.0	6.7	2,200
Married with less than two children	23.5	36.4	18,639
Married with two or more children	20.9	32.8	19,796
Major income source: property	28.4	9.4	26,279
Adjusted family income: $1,500–$15,000	26.7	6.5	1,642
Adjusted family income: $15,000 and over	32.5	2.9	24,637

Source: Computed from the MERGE data file. Because income and taxes change under each incidence assumption, the unweighted number of cases eligible for the analysis differed under each variant. For an explanation of the incidence variant, see Table 3-1. Details may not add to totals because of rounding.

a. The average effective rate shown for the total sample differs from that shown earlier in the book because it is calculated here as a weighted average of the effective tax rates of the various subgroups. The effective tax rates presented earlier were calculated by dividing total taxes by total income.

b. The stability of the estimates is inversely related to the number of cases on which they are based.

major income source was property and whose total adjusted family income was $15,000 or more.[5]

The homeowner-renter variable was included as a potential predictor in the analysis, but was not sufficiently important for explaining differences in effective tax rates. The reason is that homeownership and marital status are so highly correlated that once marital status and family size have been taken into account, housing status explains little of the remaining variation in tax rates. Similarly because age and receipts of transfer payments are highly correlated, once transfers have been used as the major income source, the age of the family head contributes little to explaining differences in tax rates.

The AID analysis confirms the basic conclusion of this book that

[5] This would correspond to approximately the highest 20 percent of the population. (See Table 4-5.)

effective tax rates are proportional throughout most of the income scale. Although the program could have chosen fairly narrow income ranges, only income of $15,000 and over was important in explaining tax rate variations—and then only for property income recipients. The urban-rural place of residence did not explain a sufficient amount of the difference in effective tax rates to be included in the results.

Variant 3b results. As is indicated in Table D-2, most of the same variables that were important in explaining differences in tax rates under Variant 1c were also included in the Variant 3b results. The major differences are the order in which the explanatory variables were used (which indicates relative importance), and the split on families with low incomes prior to that on major income source. In addition, the urban or rural place of residence was included for low-income families whose major source of income was wages.

TABLE D-2. Factors Associated with Differences in Effective Tax Rates, Incidence Variant 3b, 1966

Explanatory variable	Average effective tax rate (percent)[a]	Number of cases as a weighted percentage of entire sample	Unweighted number of cases[b]
Entire sample	26.7	100.0	71,806
Adjusted family income: under $1,500	50.4	4.7	1,755
Major income source: wages or transfers	38.9	4.0	1,534
Major income source: wages	47.3	1.5	585
Urban residents	52.4	1.0	415
Single	43.2	0.5	164
Married	62.2	0.5	251
Rural residents	34.9	0.4	170
Major income source: transfers	34.0	2.5	949
Major income source: business or property	119.1	0.7	221
Adjusted family income: $1,500 or more	25.5	95.3	70,051
Major income source: wages, business, or property	25.9	85.4	66,892
Single or married with less than two children	27.0	51.7	39,889
Single	30.0	7.6	5,667
Married with less than two children	26.5	44.1	34,222
Married with two or more children	24.3	33.8	27,003
Major income source: transfers	21.8	9.9	3,159

Source: See Table D-1. Details may not add to totals because of rounding.

a The average effective rate shown for the total sample differs from that shown earlier in the book because it is calculated here as a weighted average of the effective tax rates of the various subgroups. The effective tax rates presented earlier were calculated by dividing total taxes by total income.

b The stability of the estimates is inversely related to the number of cases on which they are based.

In the Variant 3b analysis, very low adjusted family income was the most important factor in explaining the differences in effective tax rates. Following that, in order of importance for those with incomes of $1,500 or more, were major income source and marital status. The highest effective tax rates were paid by single persons with more than $1,500 of AFI whose major income source was not from transfers. Unlike the 1c results, having property as the major income source did not contribute significantly to explaining tax rate differentials. The same factors, plus urban-rural place of residence, were important in explaining tax rates of the low-income families, but, as Table D-2 shows, the order of importance differed somewhat from that for higher-income units.

The most significant difference between the Variants 1c and 3b analyses is the split in 1c on high-income families with property income. Tax rates are relatively high for this group because the corporate tax and the property tax are allocated to owners of capital under 1c. Rates are considerably lower for those at the bottom of the income scale under 1c than under 3b, because in the latter variant half the corporation income tax and the urban property tax on improvements were allocated in proportion to consumption and housing expenditures (which are relatively highest at the bottom of the income scale). For example, for those having incomes under $1,500 and whose major source of income is wages, the average effective rate under 1c is 31.1 percent while under 3b the rate for such families is 47.3 percent. As in 1c, the housing tenure variable was not sufficiently important to enter the AID analysis after all the other factors had been included.

For most families, both of the AID analyses indicate a lack of significant difference in effective rates among those whose major income source is wages or business income. As in the case of other variables not used for splits in the analyses, the preceding explanatory variables were sufficient to explain the differences in effective rates among various family units.

Index